Veils of Power: From the Tem … Illuminati

THE ILLUMIN…

The Spark That Terrified Empires

By Julian Rothmere

Table of Contents

Series Introduction

Veils of Power: From the Templars to the Illuminati

For centuries, whispers of secret brotherhoods have haunted the edges of history. Knights, philosophers, scholars, and dreamers—all bound by silence and vision—shaped ideas that still echo in our world today.

Veils of Power is a journey through those hidden corridors of influence. From the crusading orders of medieval Europe to the shadowy societies of the Enlightenment, and finally into the modern age of digital myths, each volume uncovers how secrecy, faith, and ambition intertwined to forge legends that refuse to die.
But this is not a tale of fantasy. It is the story of how *belief*—in symbols, rituals, and invisible hierarchies—has repeatedly altered the course of power.

Each brotherhood left its mark: in stone cathedrals, in coded manifestos, in political revolutions, and in the endless fascination of the human mind with what lies unseen. Through these six volumes, you will move from fact to myth, from documentation to speculation, tracing how real men and women became icons of conspiracy.

Read them in sequence for a sweeping historical saga—or explore them individually as self-contained revelations. Either way, prepare to enter a world where history hides behind ritual, and where every truth casts a shadow.

Welcome to the journey behind the world's oldest secrets—beyond the veil of power.

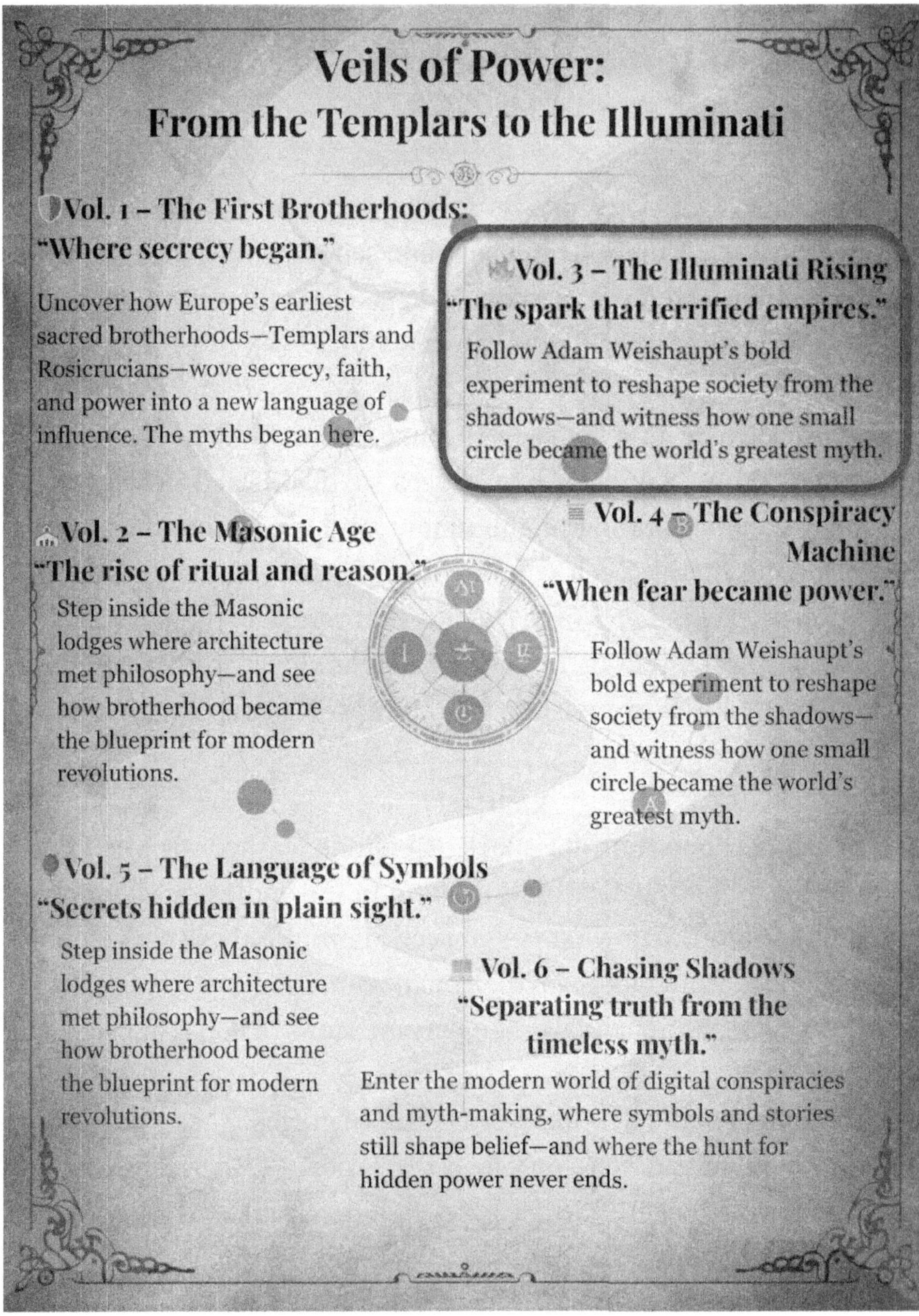

Introduction

Bavaria in 1776: an age of reason and repression

In 1776, Bavaria stood at a precarious crossroads, a patchwork of illuminated minds and shadowed hearts. The Enlightenment had swept through Europe like a wildfire, igniting the thoughts of the learned and the curious. Yet as ideas of liberty, reason, and individualism bubbled to the surface, a grim reality simmered beneath. The stark contrast between burgeoning thought and oppressive authority played out on cobblestone streets, echoing in the hushed whispers of salons and church pews alike.

To understand this paradox, one must first look beyond the glimmering façade of intellectual salons, where philosophers and poets engaged in spirited debates. It was a climate ripe with the promise of reason. Thinkers like Immanuel Kant and Johann Gottlieb Fichte challenged the foundations of society, questioning the very essence of authority and human existence. Their words, often wrapped in the elegant poetry of rational thought, hung in the air, inviting countless students to grapple with new ideas. Each parlor conversation flickered with the potential to spark a revolution—a revolution not of arms, but of intellect.

Yet, lurking behind every exchange was the tightening grip of repression. The Bavarian Electorate, ensconced in opulent palaces, viewed this burgeoning tide of thought with trepidation. Within the corridors of power, the echoes of the past held a tight leash on the present. Censorship loomed ominously over innovative publications, stifling voices that might disrupt the carefully curated narrative of order and obedience. Under the watchful eye of the state, dissenters faced exile, imprisonment, or worse—a fate not lost on those daring enough to challenge the status quo. The irony was stark; while the Age of Reason beckoned intellectual curiosity, the fist of autocracy stood poised to crush it.

Within this stifling environment, one figure began to emerge—a professor of canon law at the University of Ingolstadt named Adam Weishaupt. Weishaupt, marked by both ambition and discontent, sought to lay the foundations of a new order. Beneath the candlelight of his study, he grappled not just with the tenets of rationalism but with a deeper yearning for liberation from the chains of dogma. This conflict—between the exhilarating promise of enlightenment and the heavy hand of repression—would set him on a perilous path.

Imagine Weishaupt, hunched over a desk scattered with parchment, ink stains pooling like dark secrets on the wood. His mind raced through constellations of ideas, a restless quest for knowledge and meaning. From the oppressive fabric of religion and state, he was driven to craft a society built on reason, where individuals could explore the uncharted territories of freedom. It was beneath this polished surface of academic rigor that his revolutionary ambitions began to take shape.

Yet, as with all great revolutions, the road to liberation is marred by turmoil. The very act of seeking knowledge posed a risk. Weishaupt's initial appearances among the elite circles of Bavaria belied a fierce resolve hidden within. He courted danger with every gathering of like-minded souls, crafting not just a philosophy but a clandestine network—the Illuminati. His vision was seductive: an organization free from conformity, where merit and reason triumphed over inherited privilege. The gleam of possibility shone brightly, but shadows loomed.

What Weishaupt did not anticipate, however, was the swift backlash exacerbated by the tightening grip of authorities. As these new ideas rallied minds, they also crystallized fear in the hearts of those who governed. Envy mixed with paranoia, giving rise to sinister plots and whispers of insurrection. The state, with its machinery of oppression, scrutinized every gathering, every printed word as though it were a dagger poised at its throat.

This precarious dance of intellect and repression reached a fever pitch in Bavaria in 1776. As men of thought gathered in dimly lit salons to debate the nature of freedom, the harsh reality lingered like a storm cloud. Few could have known that the seed Weishaupt planted, vowing to cultivate a society defined by reason, would soon resonate through the ages—a challenge to the status quo that would mingle with fear, distrust, and the heady promise of revolution.

The events of 1776 mark not just the rise of ideas, but the birth of a movement grounded in the turmoil of its time. Weishaupt was not merely crafting a philosophical debate—he was readying a rebellion, one that would spark both fascination and dread. Underlined by this tumultuous landscape of Bavaria, the die was cast for a secret order that would defy conventional narratives and challenge the very foundations of society.

Before it all unraveled into myth and conspiracy, there lingered a potent mixture of hope and uncertainty. In that moment, within the crossroads of reason and repression, the Illuminati awaited their time, betting on the unpredictable nature of the human spirit. It is here, at this intersection, that the true story of the Illuminati begins—not as mere puppeteers of world events, but as brave souls willing to reconceptualize the very fabric of human understanding. The challenge was not just to think differently but to navigate the treacherous waters of an age determined to silence them. Thus, we delve deeper into their world, where shadows obscure truth and the quest for understanding becomes a battleground for the soul.

Adam Weishaupt: a radical professor's vision

In the cloistered halls of the University of Ingolstadt, Adam Weishaupt—once a zealous Jesuit—was anything but typical. Caught in a web of Enlightenment thought and deeply aware of the age's revolutionary undercurrents, he sought not merely to educate but to transform. Below the polished surface of academic rigor, a radical vision was brewing, igniting his ambition to upend societal norms. He envisioned a world where reason reigned supreme, liberated from religious dogma and tyranny, where ideas could flow freely among men of intellect. What he birthed, however, was something far stranger than mere philosophical musings: it was a clandestine fraternity aimed at reshaping the very foundations of society.

The year was 1776, a pivotal moment not only across the Atlantic but also within the weathered stone walls of his Bavarian study. A time when the multiplicative forces of revolution and reason collided. While revolutionaries in America drafted tomes declaring their independence, Weishaupt's ambitions were equally grand but utterly different. He wasn't seeking land or sovereignty; rather, he aimed for the conquest of minds. Illuminated not by lanterns but by the fiery glow of Enlightenment, he embraced the radical doctrine of promoting knowledge as a catalyst for change—a "philosophically enlightened" society. He sought to cultivate a cadre of intellectuals who could infiltrate all levels of society—an order that would work symbiotically beneath the surface, influencing decisions through dialogue rather than decree.

Yet beneath Weishaupt's vision, the path was fraught with contradictions. His aspirations echoed those of other reformers, but they were steeped in an insatiable thirst for power, emulating the very systems he wished to dismantle. He sought not just allies but acolytes—followers who would pledge their fidelity, thwarting the conventional while abiding by the unconventional. Layers upon layers of secrecy adorned his ambitions, as obscure rites and enigmatic symbols permeated the fabric of his clandestine Illuminati. True liberation, after all, must sprout from the shadows.

One must wonder: did Weishaupt realize the Pandora's box he was prying open? In forming a network of clandestine operatives, he drew a curious line between freedom and fanaticism. When managing this paradox, he walked a tightrope: any miscalculation could lead to catastrophe—not just for himself but for the societal fabric he sought to weave. Yet, despite the lurking peril, he reveled in transgression, believing that a select few had the capacity to wield knowledge as a weapon—and so, the Illuminati emerged, cloaked in secrecy.

The allure of the Illuminati was irresistible to those disillusioned by the era's stifling norms. Intellectuals, poets, and thinkers rushed to embrace Weishaupt's vision, captivated by a promise of enlightenment that rippled through the still waters of social order.

Each member became both a disciple and a conspirator, seduced by the notion that they belonged to something greater—a revolution of intellect against ignorance.

Yet as membership swelled, the ideals began to fray. Control was paramount in Weishaupt's vision; the rituals that once fostered brotherhood began to take on a sinister edge, hinting at coercion over camaraderie. The brotherhood that bloomed in secrecy found itself ensnared by its own machinations, resulting in an ideology that diverged sharply from its original aspiration. As Enlightenment thinkers sought transparency and rational discourse, the Illuminati's impenetrability became its very essence, fueling rumors of hidden agendas far more nefarious than any plebeian could fathom.

As history would later reveal, the Illuminati were not mere puppeteers of life strings, pulling for control. They became a bogeyman lurking in the corners of consciousness—fearful whispers propelling conspiracy theories that would endure for centuries. Beneath the hysteria, however, lay the haunting realization of a basic but harrowing truth: ideology becomes most dangerous and distorted in the hands of those who forget its inception. They took Weishaupt's ideals and turned them into phantoms, distorting a noble cause into a nightmarish vision of control.

In the end, Weishaupt's radical vision shifted the landscape of political thought and secret societies, igniting flames that would flicker ominously throughout the ages. While he yearned for an intellectual communion founded on shared ideals, his legacy reminded us: revolutions of the mind can quickly tangle with the desires of the heart. What started as a shared dream of enlightenment morphed into a cautionary tale, one that resonates through the corridors of history, urging us to examine closely the costs of our ideologies. Before it all unraveled, Weishaupt tapped into a truth that still whispers to us today—knowledge without transparency is but a gilded cage.

Why this story still matters: fact vs. fantasy

We exist in a society enamored with spectacle, cloaked in shadows and shrouded in myth. The Illuminati, drenched in fantastical narratives, has evolved from a confounding Bavarian fraternity into an all-encompassing archetype of conspiracy. Beneath the polished surface of these tales lies a potent truth; a truth that echoes louder today than ever before. The examination of this story transcends mere curiosity—it challenges the very fibers of our understanding of power, control, and the exchange of ideas in the modern world.

To grasp why this tale still resonates, we must first peel back the layers of fiction spun by sensationalists. The common portrait painted of the Illuminati portrays a greedy cabal haunting the halls of extraordinary wealth, orchestrating events from the shadows. This narrative is intoxicating and alluring, but irritatingly simplistic. At its inception in 1776, the Illuminati was far from nefarious; instead, it sought to harness Enlightenment ideals, advocating reason and personal liberty amidst the chaos of dogma. In an era when established authorities wielded their power with divine right, Weishaupt's ambition was to carve a space for rational discourse. Yet he too was swept up in the currents of his time—a curious blend of enlightenment and enlightenment's pitfalls.

Consider this: why are we so captivated by the idea that secret societies manipulate history from a distance? Perhaps it reflects our own disempowerment in the face of vast, impersonal forces that shape our lives. The allure of a shadowy cabal suggests answers to the chaotic questions of existence, filling the void where complexity and uncertainty loom large. The very existence of the Illuminati itself reveals an unsettling truth about human nature—our collective yearning to identify the villains behind life's tumult. In our quest for clarity, we often retreat into narratives laced with conspiracy, cloaked in intrigue. But we neglect the simpler, and perhaps more unsettling reality: history unfolds through a multitude of actors, each with their agendas, frailties, and limitations.

Before it all unraveled, the Illuminati served as both an ideology and a mirror. It reflected our revolutionary angst, our hopes for human progress, and ultimately our fears of relinquishing control. Rather than a villainous conspiracy, Weishaupt's fraternity represents a cautionary tale; an earnest—and ultimately futile—effort to combat the very forces of suppression that the revolutionaries sought to overcome. What began as an intellectual exercise in freedom morphed, as the years wore on, into a chilling narrative that utilized the cloak of secrecy for its own survival. By tracking this metamorphosis, we delve into the heart of our societal dynamics: how the narratives we embrace can warp and distort reality.

The astonishing fact is that the Illuminati, with all its glamour and peril, still matters today because it serves as a catalyst for our examination of the ideologies governing our lives. The notion of hidden powers choreographing our fate is not limited to a secret society; it permeates modern political discourse, media sensations, and, indeed, our own self-conceptions. We grapple with the crushing weight of legacy, ever fearful that we are mere puppets in a game we do not perceive. In our age of fractured attention and rampant disinformation, the fascination with the Illuminati becomes a backdrop against which we measure our own agency—or the lack thereof.

In the dystopian fabric of contemporary culture, the discussion around the Illuminati challenges our acceptance of mainstream narratives. What we once dismissed as fringe ideology now finds its roots sprouting in our communal consciousness. The conspiratorial mind, nurtured by a history of exclusion and mistrust, finds solace in these urban legends, fashioning a barbed shield against the chaotic whispers of policy and governance. It is both a cautionary tale of intellectual overreach, dependent on flimsy foundations, and a prophetic reminder of the perils of ideological extremism. Thus, understanding the Illuminati isn't merely an exercise in historical analysis; it's a crucial reflection on how we delineate fact from fantasy, motive from means.

Ultimately, the story of the Illuminati is compelling not solely for its historical ramifications but for its persistent relevance in contemporary discourse. Each rumination on the Illuminati serves as a mirror reflecting our insecurities, our rebellion against the unknown, and our grappling with the forces that shape our lives, often invisibly. To dismiss this narrative as mere fiction is to lose sight of the evolving complexities of power. As we forge our path through the intertwined landscapes of ideology and reality, we must remain vigilant. History is, after all, most dangerous when we stop checking the footnotes. So, let us turn the page towards understanding, as we unravel the story that brought us here, a tale that beckons us to check our assumptions and engage with the truths we often overlook.

Chapter 1: Seeds of Revolution

The Enlightenment in Germany

In the sweeping embrace of the 18th century, Germany stood poised, a crucible of thought yet to be ignited. Beneath the polished surface of its burgeoning universities and aristocratic salons, the ideological currents of the Enlightenment twisted and turned with a wild urgency. This was an era pregnant with ideas, where the dense fog of dogma began to lift, revealing a new landscape ripe for exploration. For intellectuals like Immanuel Kant and Johann Gottlieb Fichte, the very act of thinking was a revolutionary act, a rebellion against centuries of entrenched authority.

Imagine the cobblestone streets of Königsberg, where Kant meticulously honed his thoughts on autonomy and morality—a breathtaking collision of reason wrapped in the mundane rhythm of a provincial city. There, beneath the quaint façades, lay the once-unthinkable proposition that humans could learn to pursue reason over tradition, that enlightenment could arise not just from the royal decree but from the mind of the individual. Kant's "What is Enlightenment?" posed a question that rippled through the hearts of many—a rallying cry for the spirited young intellectuals craving emancipation from the shackles of their past.

The air resonated with the fervor of change, a cacophony of fresh voices advocating for human rights, dignity, and self-governance. Think of the fierce debates echoing through the lecture halls where Hegel articulated his vision of a reconciled world, shaped and reshaped by the dialectic tension of thesis and antithesis.

Revolutionary, visionary, but also deeply flawed, he traversed the landscape of history with an optimism that was both intoxicating and bewildering—a promise that the march towards freedom was inevitable, even if it demanded tremendous sacrifice.

Yet even as the lights of reason shone bright, shadows lingered in the corners, where the specters of conformity and dogmatism awaited. Frederick the Great's Prussia operated under an enlightened despotism, an intriguing dichotomy where the king indulged the philosophies of the Enlightenment while ruthlessly suppressing any hint of rebellion. Here lay a paradox that would surface again and again: the revolutionary ideas championed within gilded walls were often shackled by the iron grip of those in power, who feared what they could not control.

As discontent simmered across the continent, the fray of Enlightenment thought tugged at the seams of society. The salons of Berlin infused life into this longing for change—vigorous discussions over clinking glasses of wine and the soft hush of candlelight illuminated the pages of history. Figures like Henriette Herz and Rahel Varnhagen gathered the intellectual elite, an eclectic mix of philosophers, poets, and often fervent skeptics. It was here that Friedrich Schiller and his theatrical genius blossomed, capable of capturing not just the sociopolitical climates of their time but the visceral passions that drove humanity itself.

Behind the discussions of lofty ideals, however, a darker tale unfolded. The more radical thinkers, those who truly wished to break away from tradition, found themselves at odds not just with authority, but with society itself. The tension between progressive thought and reactionary restraint crackled like a storm about to break. It was within this quagmire of thought that a clandestine path began to take form, a hidden society that promised to safeguard the revolutionary tenets of the Enlightenment—a mission borne out of necessity.

In the hallowed halls of faculties and lecture rooms, Adam Weishaupt, a disillusioned Jesuit trained in the dark arts of philosophy, stumbled upon the idea that would burgeon into the Illuminati. His convictions were infused with a pure urgency, an understanding that individual enlightenment was critical, but collective enlightenment—an orchestration of the intellectual elite—could upend the entire societal structure.

He was an intellectual knight, armed with notions of liberty and equality, yet acutely aware of the tightening noose of ignorance that swayed the masses. The very idea of a brotherhood dedicated to advancing enlightenment, unencumbered by the shackles of factionalism, glimmered before him—a beacon against the encroaching darkness of dogmatism.

But Weishaupt's vision was not just revolutionary; it was dangerously naïve. The notion that philosophy could outmaneuver the brutal realities of politics and power would soon unravel, revealing an ugly truth: societies hesitant to embrace intellectual freedom were invariably quick to silence dissenting voices. The complexity of human nature—its capacity for both altruism and egotism—remained as potent a force as any ideology, perhaps more so. Beneath the hopeful veneer of enlightenment, the problems of a society enthralled by hierarchy and privilege loomed large, often crushing those who dared to pursue a different path.

Then came the storm—a gale of dissension blew through Germany, shaking the foundation of Enlightenment ideals. The French Revolution ignited passions across Europe, illuminating a stark contrast: while revolutions promised liberty, they often delivered the blood-soaked chaos of tyranny. Glaring contradictions emerged; the ideologies advocated in hushed salons echoed hollowly against the screams of disillusioned masses. German intellectuals wrestled with their identities, teetering between unyielding loyalty to tradition and the zealous embrace of radical change.

The stage was set for a confrontation between ideology and reality, between the sanitized aesthetics of thought and the brutal complexities of human existence. The Enlightenment, once a delicate flower of reason, became an unstable reaction subject to the whims of those who clung to the old orders. The ramifications of this ideological tension would remain ingrained in the very heart of the Illuminati's mission, an endeavor to reconcile the ideal with the actual—a Sisyphean task fraught with inherent contradictions.

As one gazes back through the fog of history, the irony of it all lies in the unrelenting pursuit of truth amid a world steeped in obfuscation and denial. The Enlightenment forged paths toward idealism that would flicker only to be doused by hands less noble. Herrschaft over the intellectual and the spirit of inquiry clashed with the brutal force of control, creating a play that would eventually lift the veil on secrets even the brightest minds couldn't fully fathom.

Thus, the seeds of revolution did not merely sprout from lofty principles; they were intricately woven from the very fabric of human experience—the pursuit of knowledge, the desire for liberty, and the harsh reality of confrontation with the tyrannies of both thought and governance. In the heart of Germany, where the intellect thrived, the soul of revolution simmered with exquisite inevitability, waiting to burst forth amid the contradictions and chaos. As we peel back the layers of Enlightenment's complex legacy, we will find that the struggle for genuine enlightenment has only just begun.

Why Weishaupt rejected church and monarchy

In the shadowy corridors of Renaissance thought, where reason began to wrestle with faith, Adam Weishaupt found himself shackled by the weight of tradition—anxious priests and unyielding monarchs, stewards of a divine order that stifled any flicker of dissent. As the glimmer of Enlightenment dawned on Europe, it shone a light on the cavernous depths of hypocrisy that lurked within established institutions. The church, with its iron grip on morals and doctrine, stood in stark contrast to the burgeoning ideals of reason and liberty. Weishaupt, a scion of Bavarian academia, rejected these dogmas not out of simple rebellion, but out of a fervent desire for an enlightened society unfettered by the chains of superstition and tyranny.

Beneath the polished surface of this intellectual uprising, he readied himself to take on the twin pillars of oppression: the ecclesiastical authority that preached salvation while suffocating inquiry, and the monarchy, whose dazzling robes concealed a deep-seated fear of knowledge. The church professed eternal truths, yet clung to temporal power with a ferocity that belied its divine claims. Monarchical rule, draped in the regalia of divine right, struck down any whisper of reform, lest the throne tremble beneath the weight of reasoned argument.

In the heart of Bavaria, amidst the tepid pedantry of his contemporaries, Weishaupt cultivated a vision—one where man would no longer bow before the altar of sovereign authority or the cathedral's imposing façade. He envisioned a society where individuals could explore the realms of knowledge free from the dogma that shackled their ancestors. His rejection of church and monarchy was, at its core, a radical affirmation of human potential. What was salvation, he questioned, if it came at the cost of one's ability to think independently? What was kingship, if it silenced the voice of rationality?

His academic milieu, rife with specimens of Enlightenment thought, provided a fertile ground for rebellion. In those early debates over coffee and manuscripts, the likes of Rousseau and Locke fueled his growing disillusionment. Weishaupt savored their daring challenge to the status quo—a call to arms for the oppressed and the overlooked. The idea echoed within him: a society governed by laws rooted in reason rather than the whims of a crown or the shallow promises of a priest. But as exhilarating as this epiphany was, it was tempered by an acute awareness of the risks involved. The Church had executed dissenters in glorious spectacles, and monarchs regarded reform as treason.

Yet, what lay before Weishaupt was more than mere defiance; it was the birth of a philosophy—a radical worldview that shook the very foundation of 18th-century society. His rejection of the church and monarchy was woven with personal conviction, yet it also echoed the collective anxiety bruising an era on the verge of explosion. The voices of the marginalized, the cries for liberty from men and women imprisoned by expectation—all clamored for a revolutionary manifesto.

Before it all unraveled, a moment of chiaroscuro revealed itself in the annals of history: January 1776, the cusp of the American Revolution, and here was Weishaupt, pen poised, burning with the fervor of ideas that transcended borders. He understood the stakes: forging a doctrine that could galvanize thinkers and visionaries alike, uniting them under an ethos of Enlightenment ideals. It was a precarious venture, balancing the passionate right to freedom against the dogged preservation of authority. The stakes were inextricably high; for Weishaupt, failure meant losing everything—his life, his vision, and the promise of a society he believed was within reach.

Thus emerged the Illuminati, studded with enlightened principles, instrumental and keenly aware of the discourse of power. Their agenda ruptured not just the medieval chains of authority but sought to obliterate the illusions of infallibility that bound them. The pathos of Weishaupt's decision echoed throughout the fledgling chapters of the Illuminati: to navigate the labyrinth of power without replicating the oppressive structures they sought to dismantle. To act in defiance was one thing; to do so while remaining honorable to the ideals of liberty and humanity was another.

Weishaupt's clandestine society was not saturated with malice or conspiratorial longing. Rather, it brimmed with aspirations forged in sharp clarity; a tightrope walk balanced between inclusion and exclusion. Here resided the paradox of Enlightenment ideals: the noble pursuit of knowledge could also fracture the very foundations underfoot. Trust, once a currency traded upon faith, now demanded transactions governed by reason—a complex, fragile arrangement to enact radical change.

As the Illuminati took their first steps, they knew that they needed to chart a course through treacherous waters. Beneath bright banter and public camaraderie, darkened chambers echoed with disdain for the rulers who operated under archaic pretexts. Members of the order, from philosophers to politicians, debated topics far too incendiary for the open air of universities or picnic gatherings. They drew plans in the dead of night, fueled by the recognition that power lay not just in philosophy but in the networks binding them to common goals; a connective tissue that thrummed with the urgency of revolution.

In rejecting the oppressive frameworks of church and monarchy, Adam Weishaupt offered more than a critique. He advanced visions of collective action and shared knowledge—a map charted in values rooted deeply within the Enlightenment. He sought the unveiling of humanity's potential, one that transcended the inherited shackles of faith and obedience. In sharp contrast to the turbulence of revolution, he dared to embrace a course of logic amidst chaos—a pursuit grounded in the understanding that unchecked power ultimately corrupts.

Thus, the seeds of revolution germinated within Weishaupt's resolute heart: a fiery rejection of deceit wrapped in authority. He saw the gaping fissures that threatened to rend the fabric of society, and he resolved to weave together an alternative path, illuminated by the fierce light of reason. Before it all unraveled, what emerged was a vision of a fraternity dedicated to the pursuit of truth—a clarion call that rang out, echoing through the ages, even until today.

As we delve deeper into the machinations of Weishaupt's Illuminati, we begin to unravel not just the methodology of their operations, but the profound philosophical undercurrents that drove them forward—a relentless quest for a society capable of dismantling the iron fist of dogma and tyranny, one radiant idea at a time.

The idea of secret reform

The idea of secret reform is a treacherous precipice, one all too easily obscured by the fog of intentions that cloud its underlying motives. In the late 18th century, Europe simmered with the discontent of the common man, a powder keg of ideas ready to ignite beneath the polished surface of aristocratic courts and opulent cathedrals. Amid this turmoil, a new breed of intellectual emerged, advocating not for revolution in the streets, but for a quiet—often clandestine—reformation of the very foundations of society. Can we dare to behold the irony? What began as a whispered rebellion against tyranny soon transformed into a tangled web of secrecy and manipulation.

Take, for example, the figure of Adam Weishaupt, whose vision of an enlightened society sparked the fire of the Bavarian Illuminati in 1776. Weishaupt was not a soldier but a scholar, a professor of canon law at the University of Ingolstadt. His tools were not muskets and cannons but pens, ink, and a cadre of like-minded individuals hungry for intellectual upheaval. Their philosophy—a cocktail of Enlightenment ideals brewed with the darker elixirs of ambition—proposed a world unshackled from the chains of dogma and superstition. Beneath the erudite dialogues of the Illuminati's clandestine meetings lay a conviction that guiding society through intellectual enlightenment would usher in a new dawn, one governed not by the capricious whims of monarchs, but by rational discourse and collectivism.

Yet, in this welding of ideas, concern begot paranoia. What would transform these benevolent pursuits—proposed reforms and liberating philosophies—into schemes cloaked in secrecy? The very act of hiding necessitated a careful choreography of trust and betrayal, of loyalty and fear. The blatancy of reform had fallen by the wayside, and beneath it all lay a gnawing urgency to act without alerting the powerful. The paradox of reform became clear: the more desired the change, the more the reformers retreated into obscurity, allowing their noble intentions to become suffocated under layers of intrigue.

Weishaupt wasn't alone in his pursuits. An array of influential figures populated the shadows around him, caught in the magnetic pull of revolutionary thought that swayed them like leaves in a gale. Men and women gathered in corners of cafes and salons, building an ideological ecosystem that nurtured dissent. Their words flowed like wine at a banquet—inviting yet intoxicating, words that went down smooth but hummed with an underlying tension. They sought not only to dream of an ideal society but to map out how such a utopia might thrive, and they soon discovered that secrecy could be both a tool and a weapon.

Consider the freemasons, whose own organization served as both a lodge of camaraderie and an arsenal for reform. The very essence of masonry—an intricate dance of symbols, rituals, and hidden meanings—possessed an alluring quality that drew the brilliant and disenchanted alike. It was here that ideas bounced in echoes off the walls, illuminating the shadows and sparking imaginations. But veiled beneath these rituals lay a dangerous interplay of influence and control, a paradox that pitted their collective goals against the desire to remain unobserved by the watchful eyes of the powerful.

In the dimly lit corners of these lodges, urgent discussions tore away at the veneer of monarchy. Yet, such secretive parlance came at a price. The urgency for reform often spiraled into an obsession with the elite and the establishment, a desperate desire to wrest control from their iron grasp. It became an ideological arms race where the more they plotted, the more vulnerable they became to exposure. Before long, the very secrecy that promised salvation morphed into a source of distrust, carefully cultivated by those who feared losing grips on their dominions.

And just as the revolutionary fervor grew, so did the echoing silence of dissent within the ranks. Many feared the implications of Weishaupt's aspirations, sensing the potential for his radicalism to shift the balance from enlightenment to tyranny—a betrayal of the very ideals they sought to uphold. The Enlightenment discourse, once vibrant and brimming with promise, soon began to congeal into a cautious whisper of unease regarding the appropriateness of veiled approaches to reform.

In a way, the movement became a reflection of its own geopolitical landscape, a mirror to the darker recesses of human ambition. Nations were redefining themselves at a breathtaking pace, principles that once motivated exploration and discovery now steered into the murky waters of ambition cloaked in secrecy. In the heart of the Bavarian experiment, where reason was to surge forth as a cleansing flood, Weishaupt instead found himself vying for momentum amid the swirling chaos of political intrigue and hidden agendas.

It raises the question: Is reform best approached in daylight or darkness? A nostalgic longing for heroic reform haunted those who fled into secrecy, yet the origins of their noble intentions lay buried within layers of deception. As the currents of history surged onward, we must wonder how many opportunities for rightful change were discarded in the shadows. The idea of secret reform, birthed in idealism, consistently grapples with its own twisted potential—one that offers both elevation and demise.

History judges harshly. Within the tapestry of the Enlightenment, what was once a promise of salvation had, in many ways, devolved into a cautionary tale. The balance between radical thought and clandestine behavior became precarious, leaving an indelible imprint on the revolutionary narrative. Before it all unraveled, the silent promoters of change had to reckon with the innate contradictions of their cause, the unrelenting tension bubbling beneath the surface of whispered conversations.

In the end, it is vital to discern between the purpose and the pathway to that purpose in the annals of secret reform. Ideas may burgeon in the dark, but can real change endure shadows that twist the very intentions that birthed them? The struggle between openness and secrecy remains a haunting refrain echoing through history—a paradox where dreams for a better world teeter perilously on the brink of ambition gone awry. With each puzzle piece added, we inch closer to understanding the Illuminati not just as players of a secretive game, but as harbingers of the very human struggle for truth amidst a labyrinth of ideology.

Chapter 2: Founding the Illuminati

The secret tavern meeting of 1776

In the summer of 1776, as the ink dried on the Declaration of Independence and America flickered to life, a secret meeting took place beneath the gaudy chandeliers of a nondescript tavern tucked away in the heart of Ingolstadt. The air, thick with the scented smoke of burning pipe tobacco and the rasp of half-drunk laughter, belied the gravity of the discussions unfolding within. Here, in a candle-lit corner hidden from prying eyes, flickered the initial sparks of what would become an exhilarating but troubling ideological journey—the founding of the Illuminati.

It was a clandestine gathering of minds gravitating toward the radical. Illuminated souls, if you will, eager to chart alternative realms of thought amidst a backdrop of rising oppression and intellectual fervor. At the helm was Adam Weishaupt, the primary architect of this eager confabulation, a professor at the University of Ingolstadt. A man whose reputation as a radical thinker danced on the precipice of treason. Beneath the polished surface of those intellectual debates lay a potent mix of philosophy and ambition—a cocktail as intoxicating as the beer frothing in their mugs.

The tavern, with its low ceiling and heavy oak beams, offered refuge to revolutionaries not merely of the political kind but of the mind. Among the attendees were some of the period's frenetic thinkers: writers grappling with Enlightenment ideals, free thinkers challenging established dogmas, and fervent reformists demanding a more equitable society. They huddled conspiratorially; each one animated by an ethical outrage concealed beneath the guise of merriment. Numerous voices rose and fell like the tides, with the raucous clinking of glasses punctuating the passionate discussions.

"We must craft a new society," Weishaupt opined decisively, his eyes aflame with the zeal of a prophet. "One where knowledge reigns supreme and ignorance stands condemned." The words fell like stones into stagnant waters, rippling across syntheses of thought—progressive notions of liberty coupled with an unsettling rhetoric that pointed toward a detachment from tradition. His proposition struck chords of resonance that often shattered the air with applause.

Yet, doubts loomed, shadows intermingling with the candles' flickering glow. The question loomed large: could such lofty ideals survive the weight of tradition? Beneath the heady intoxication of radical ideas, flickered the specter of failure, whispering of possible betrayals from within. The burgeoning desire for revolution might be a scorched path, littered with the remnants of broken principles.

By dissecting the fabric of existing social orders, those gathered began dissecting their own identities. Who were they in the grand scheme of things? Scholars seeking to eliminate ignorance? Or mere disbanded souls peering out from the crevasses of a society they had long felt estranged from? The atmosphere grew electric, charged with unarticulated aspirations, suggestions flitting through the air like lightning bolts. What began as merriment evolved into fierce proclamations of unity that bordered on cultish fervor—an unsettling mix that would change the course of history.

Weishaupt's influence transformed the tavern into a stage for the manipulation of ideology, drawing men and women alike into his literate whirlpool. Destination: uncertainty. Between frenzied discussions about creating a society rooted in meritocracy and fraternity, the resulting dialectic demanded action. From this gathering emerged a stress-tested philosophy that would question the essence of authority itself, even when set against the forging fires of history.

The raucous laughter cloaked beneath the tavern's worn beams stood in sharp contrast to the emerging cognitive dissonance within. Here, the battle between knowledge and ignorance spilled over into the realm of music and speech, yet tended toward a rationale only a few could grasp fully. In the shadows of every fleeting jest lingered the potential for upheaval significant enough to shake society's very foundations. The stakes were high, the ambitions great, but the growing fear of repercussions became palpable.

As discussions turned philosophical—free will versus determinism, the essence of morality as it navigated through unchecked ambition—the gathering understood that their collective fate might rest precariously on a foundation layered in secrecy and fervor. The irony remained unmissed; in their quest for enlightenment, they danced on the edge of an abyss of potential nihilism.

With the candles guttering low and the tavern's atmosphere heavy with camaraderie, oaths of loyalty were exchanged—not only to each other but also to ideas forged in the fires of rebellion. An unusual friendship blossomed amid the promises of progress: rich, intoxicating, fraught with undertones of betrayal. It echoed in the cries of "liberté" that rolled off the tongues of revolutionaries beyond the confines of Bavaria. Weishaupt held a vision spiraling outwards, pushing against the boundaries of academia and morality into uncharted territory.

Yet, as they tossed back ale, eyes glimmering with ambition, few suspected that the fruit of their labor could, and ultimately would, sow discord amongst the very ranks they venerated. Reality, strikingly sobering, would eventually reveal that ideologies, regardless of their eloquence, carried with them an inherent fragility.

What began in that tavern would unfold into a web of influence and power, stretching far beyond the confines of Bavaria. The Illuminati would not remain a secret club of intellectual revelers. No, they would soon become players on an unpredictable board of history, surrounded by a society terrified of disruptive ideas. Their ethos captured the power of thought—so revolutionary that it intimidated governments, instigated conspiracies, and fashioned a myth guarding the club like an ever-watchful spirit of the night.

So, when the tavern's patrons left that evening, they carried more than just the taste of bitterness on their lips. The reckoning—a mingling of idealism and reality—cast long shadows before them. Before history would move ahead, it would crunch beneath the weight of ambition, exposing the fissures between intentions and consequences.

And only then would it become apparent that the journey had indeed begun, traversing a delicate path between enlightenment and insurrection, yearning for a world where darkness had been the governing paradigm. With that tavern meeting, the Illuminati was born—an idea wrapped in an enigma, brimming with promise but hovering perilously close to the edge of a chasm.

First members, rituals, and early danger

Beneath the polished surface of Enlightenment ideals, a tumultuous sea of ambition and ideology roiled. In the dimly lit circles of Ingolstadt, eager minds began to stir, drawn together by a shared thirst for knowledge that was as intoxicating as it was perilous. The very first members of Adam Weishaupt's audacious venture were not mere academics; they were purveyors of an idea that threatened the very foundations of societal harmony. These men—philosophers, aspiring intellects, and disenchanted clerics—found kinship in the shadows, where power lay dormant and the seeds of a new order awaited fertile ground.

The year was 1776, and the world outside echoed with the clatter of revolutions, both political and philosophical. As throngs of thinkers penned treatises on liberty, the early members of the Illuminati clamored for a path that diverged sharply from the tumultuous rhetoric of rebellion. They sought enlightenment, not through the fires of war, but through intellectual subversion. It was in these sacred spaces—small gathering rooms in quiet taverns, candlelit schools, and secluded study halls—that the seeds of the Bavarian Illuminati were sown, nurtured by clandestine oaths and rituals that would bind them as both comrades and conspirators.

At first glance, the rituals might appear innocuous, mere ceremonies to promote brotherhood and enlightenment. Widely misunderstood, these gatherings were not about worshiping arcane symbols or invoking dark forces; rather, they were manifestations of a radical ethos. Members practiced initiations steeped in classical philosophy, echoing the mysteries of ancient societies. The light of reason was their guiding star, yet even the brightest light casts shadows. Weishaupt understood well that transformational zeal could veer dangerously close to fanaticism.

The initiation rites concocted by Weishaupt were rich tapestries woven from the fabric of esoteric mysticism and rational thought. New members were led blindfolded through darkened halls, challenged to confront fear and uncertainty—metaphors for the tumultuous journey of acquiring knowledge itself. Only after proving their worth through trial and reflection where they unbound, stepping into a realm where their intellect would shield them from the oppressive structures of power.

Yet, the very seeds of that camaraderie lay entwined with danger. The first members could hardly afford to be naïve; the specter of their ambitions invited scrutiny. In the early days, the Illuminati's network grew slowly, constrained by an innate caution. Each recruit was meticulously vetted, scrutinized within an inch of their existence—not merely for their intellectual capacity but for their loyalty to the goals of exposing corrupt institutions. The world was unforgiving, and any misstep would invite the invasive eye of the state.

As word of these clandestine societies began to slip through the cracks, the authorities stirred in irritation. The very air trembled with the knowledge that a subtle revolution brewed underfoot, one that would not signal its presence with the clangor of swords but with the silent assembly of thoughts. Despite their attempts to remain shielded, the ominous threats loomed larger, growing as whispers spread. Within the hallowed circles of power, resentment brewed, and the rulers of Europe sensed the ripples of discontent that had begun to encroach upon their well-fortified fortresses.

Weishaupt's masterpiece—an ideological web interlinking Enlightenment thought with subversive innovation—began to fracture under the weight of its ambition. Envy and paranoia started to infect the fraternity, as not all members remained steadfast in their beliefs. Abandoning their initial spirits of camaraderie, some turned their backs, revealing secrets for the allure of safety amidst the ever-looming specter of state retribution. Their loss was not just personal; it struck at the very foundation of the organization and ignited fractures that would reverberate throughout its history.

By the autumn of 1777, that once serene optimism spiraled into turmoil. Not only did external authorities tighten their grip, but internal dissent began to eat at the heart of the Illuminati. Within weeks, rifts created a cacophony of voices that sought to pull the organization in various, often conflicting directions. Weishaupt found himself standing at the helm of a disjointed ship. The struggle for ideological purity threatened to drown out the voice of rationality. He faced a core dilemma: how far could he push this vision for illumination without provoking the very societal forces they sought to dismantle?

The shadows deepened as factionalism bred chaos, each division crystallizing into distinct ideologies, leaving the Illuminati's fundamental message muted amidst the din. Where there should have been unity within scholarly pursuits, distrust replaced amicable discourse. The early danger was not merely that of being caught—though the threat was all too real—but that revolution would turn upon itself, devouring its progenitors. Before it all unraveled,

Weishaupt challenged his comrades to hold firm against the encroaching nihilism by reimagining their role within the societal conundrum, elevating discourse, and pursuing strength through ideas rather than combative rhetoric.

But reality was an unforgiving teacher. The stakes intensified as rival secret societies emerged, each twisting Enlightenment ideals for their own gain, each dragging the Illuminati further into the quagmire of infernal politics. The internal spats soon transitioned into a public diagnostic, with a sensational frenzy igniting not only within Bavaria but throughout Europe. The narrative became rife with concerns of conspiracies and hidden agendas—a potent cocktail that only stoked the flames of paranoia among authorities wary of subversion.

Fringe ideologies too often purport a golden future without assessing the landscape riddled with pitfalls. The Illuminati's brand of enlightenment began to fester with the knowledge that even noble thoughts could become the nexus of insidious manipulation. Each act of defiance became a potential jeopardy, whereby exposure suddenly meant obliteration. The very pursuit of illumination illuminated treachery hiding beneath the surface of camaraderie, unraveling the fabric of their revolutionary ambitions and sowing the chaotic seeds of their undoing.

As we delve further into the early chapters of the Illuminati, it remains clear that what began as a pursuit of intellectual freedom quickly morphed into a dangerous gambit, one that would test the resolve of the bravest minds in a world fiercely resistant to change. The intimate connection between ideology and reality cannot be overstated; this interplay would define not just their journey but the lasting impact of a dormant thread binding society, even when unacknowledged. Thus, we turn the page to the unfolding drama—a narrative not only of ambition but of peril, where the shadows deepen and the danger looms larger, setting the stage for an intoxicating story from which few would emerge unscathed.

The structure of the new order

The essence of the Illuminati lay not in their grand ambitions but in the covert architecture of influence they sought to assemble beneath the polished surface of enlightenment philosophy. Adam Weishaupt, an astute professor steeped in the academic vigor of the Enlightenment, understood that revolutions are most potent when they simmer out of sight, nurtured within the shadows cast by centuries of dogma and tradition. In May of 1776, amidst swirling ideas of freedom and reason, he initiated this clandestine assembly, forever entwining his fate with notions both thrilling and treacherous.

Weishaupt's intention was clear: forge a new societal construct, one that would make reason the highest arbiter of human affairs. He envisioned an intellectual elite—one perhaps too idealistic yet undeniably compelling—where philosophy and morality would be seamlessly interwoven. But these ideals required a structure, an intricate design that would shelter ambitious minds from the icy winds of superstition and unyielding authority. This was no mere fraternity; this was to be the nucleus of a revolutionary vanguard, the ember from which a flame would rise to illuminate the dark corners of society's ignorance.

Underneath the scholar's crisp exterior lay a playbook for manipulation and control. The Illuminati thrived on secrecy, a virtue not merely to shield its members from persecution but to envelop their machinations in a fog of enigma. Each cell of the organization functioned much like a burgeoning tree of knowledge, with branches extending outward, fragmenting into local conspirators, but rooted in the core edicts drafted by Weishaupt himself. This method ensured that the ideologies developed within the highest echelons would not omelet too quickly—rather, they would age in secret, cultivating strength over time.

To elucidate this, one must consider the nuanced levels of membership, cascading hierarchy, and the ritualistic nature of their gatherings. From the common initiate—often a zealous youth with aspirations but little understanding—to the "Perfectibility," the highest rank of the Illuminati, filled with a sense of divine mission and enlightenment superiority. Each member was stitched into a complex fabric of obligation and conspiracy: a binding oath sworn under the cloak of night. The immediacy with which dark desires fester could be illuminated at meetings. Yet, these gatherings were not just pathways of instruction but also arenas where symbolic gestures lurked behind the veil of enlightenment. They relished the knowledge that the greatest truths often lay hidden beneath layers of ritual, where each whisper of conspiratorial dialogue could echo for eternity.

Occasionally, their assemblies echoed with the laughter of camaraderie, but often they bore the weight of a shared burden—a recognition that their mission teetered on the gossamer edge of Greatness and Treachery. These self-selected arbiters of truth sought to embolden their resolve through shared knowledge, wherein the dualities of ambition clashed—the ideologue against the pragmatist. In traversing this chasm, the Illuminati embarked on an audacious journey fraught with ideological paradoxes. Were they not as cunning as the despots they sought to overthrow?

Taking inspiration from their radical contemporaries, the Illuminati injected the idea of reason itself as their philosophical linchpin. Their doctrine called for the dissolution of state and church, aspects equally unyielding in their power—an audacious repudiation of separation so sewn tightly within the fabric of daily life. And yet, within this ambition lay a tidy irony; to dismantle the very authorities that had kept society in check was to invite a new instability that could consume them from within. As the gears turned on this revolutionary machinery, lines blurred, revealing the fundamental question: who becomes the arbiter, and what becomes of morality itself when wielded as a tool of power?

Their networks stretched like a web, each node buzzing with a fervor that belied their heady ambitions. The illuminati had courted many notable figures—entrepreneurs, thinkers, and even those ensconced in the highest echelons of nobility. Each connection was meticulously plotted to enhance their reach within the era's precarious politics. Yet, while such alliances breathed life into their cause, they also ensnared them in a tempest—a seductive longing for legitimacy that threatened to expose their clandestine operations to those ever-vigilant guardians of tradition.

To maintain control, Weishaupt crafted an elaborate vocabulary, an analytical lexicon concealing their aims within lofty phrases. They whispered the language of freedom while carrying the heft of iron shackles. Irony dripped from their tongues: the call for liberation emanating from those who sought to redefine what it meant to be liberated—a paradox that might have made even the sagacious Socrates pause. The Illuminati constructed a dichotomy: they were defenders of reason yet practitioners of subterfuge, deploying their knowledge like weapons forged in the darkest forges of ambition.

Yet, even as they spun intricate plans under the candle-lit vaults of their secretive meetings, motives bubbled beneath the surface—a struggle between idealism and the unnatural lure of elitism. The perverse realization dawned: the desire for a new order might jeopardize the old, but it also risked forsaking the pursuit of enlightenment itself. This inherent tension saw the Illuminati dance unfurling in circles of intrigue—an interminable review of purpose and ideology versus the reality of their ambitions, much like the figures in a philosophical dialectic where progress is clouded by unresolved tensions.

To dissect the structure of this new order requires us to venture deeper. The Illuminati were not simply architects of ideology; they were curators of reality polished but flawed, a glistening façade that risked crumbling the very moment the world outside laid eyes upon it. In truth, they sought a revolution not merely of government but of the human spirit—lifting it out of the mire of mediocrity. Every revolutionary act became a small revolution of thought. As they sketched blueprints for a world reformed through rationalism, a question hovered and tainted their every move: would they ascend to the heights of their noble intention, or would they tumble into the abyss wrought by unexamined power?

Thus, it would be through this experimental lens that we see the Illuminati's quest for a new order—a tantalizing narrative of ambition, contradiction, and a ceaseless drive for domination cloaked in the garb of nobility. In the end, it begs a tougher question: when ideologies collide, when the sublime edges ever so closely with the grotesque, who truly holds the reins of enlightenment, and who merely poses as its benefactor? The answer is often found buried deep within the shadows, well beyond the glorious proclamations of freedom.

Chapter 3: Expansion and Ambition

Recruitment of students and nobles

As the smoldering embers of the Enlightenment began to glow, Adam Weishaupt discerned an opportunity below the polished surface of academia and the gilded halls of nobility. He understood that revolution didn't merely require fervor; it demanded cunning, an intricate web of alliances woven into the fabric of society. With a bold heart, he embarked on a recruitment mission that would both galvanize his cause and strategically counter the entrenched powers of the age.

Beneath the veneer of 18th-century European sophistication lay a societal landscape fraught with tensions—class disparities, intellectual yearning, and a burgeoning skepticism towards monarchies and dogmas. Weishaupt knew he needed recruits who could navigate these turbulent waters with grace and intellectual sharpness. And where better to find them than within the very institutions that shaped opinion and policy?

At the heart of the Illuminati's strategy was the university, a venerable institution that cast a long shadow over European thought. Weishaupt descended upon the halls of the University of Ingolstadt, where centuries of knowledge converged and where young minds burned with the desire to forge a new destiny. He sought those students who were more than just passively absorbing lessons—they were the seekers of truths, the questioners of authority.

It was in candlelit dorm rooms and musty libraries that Weishaupt scoured for the intellectually restless. The allure of enlightenment called to them—a siren song that spoke not only of knowledge but of greater purpose. He promised them more than mere academic accolades; he offered an invitation to shape the world. "Join us," he whispered through clandestine meetings cloaked in secrecy. "You shall unveil the veils that conceal knowledge and power. You become the architects of a new society."

For many, it was as though a door had cracked open to reveal a realm of possibilities previously unimaginable. Beneath the conservatively hushed tones of authorized curricula, fanatical debates raged. Weishaupt showcased revolutionary texts and philosophical works, illuminating radical ideas that would later send shockwaves across Europe. The Enlightenment was, after all, a veritable Pandora's box waiting to be unleashed, and he held the key.

Yet, as any would-be revolutionary can attest, merely drawing a crowd is a deceptive victory. Weishaupt required not just idealists but players of substance—those possessing the social capital and networks to affect genuine change. This need for legitimacy pushed him to the sidelines of nobility, where titles carried weight, and connections could open palace doors or slam them shut.

Navigating through the elegant gatherings and soirées of the nobility demanded a different kind of finesse. It was here that the Illuminati aimed for the upper crust of society—not just to undermine it, but to pervasively infiltrate its influence. Weishaupt's proposition was not merely one of ideology; he cast the Illuminati as a cursed-honored fraternity, a gilded cloak wrapped around an idealistic core. The balance of rationality and aristocracy.

In grand ballrooms adorned with flickering chandeliers, Weishaupt presented his vision veiled in the lustrous fabrics of political intrigue. To prospective nobles, he painted a picture of a society liberated from the shackles of superstition, where enlightened governance could elevate humanity and refine the basest of desires—ego and greed—into a collective pursuit of the greater good.

Consider, for example, the case of Baron von Knigge, a man well-schooled in the art of societal navigation, who would play a pivotal role in transforming scattered plots of ambition into a coherent doctrine. When he met Weishaupt, it was the fusion of both ambition and idealism that lit their initial interactions. Desperation for deeper connections ignited the fire that would eventually spread. Von Knigge understood the game of power; thus, when he agreed to the clandestine cause, it opened a floodgate. Through him, Weishaupt would gain access to influential salons and households across Germany.

But such recruitment was a double-edged sword. Within the vaulted walls and hallowed parlors, a singular misstep could unravel the entire fabric. The discussions mingled with glances of suspicion. Whispers of conspiracy danced from mouth to ear, and Weishaupt soon realized that among the powerful, there lay seeds of paranoia waiting to germinate. What happens when ambitious students and nobles clash? Most often, the dreamer wakes to find their grand ambitions scattered like autumn leaves in the wind.

Consider the gambit's emotional undercurrents. What must it feel like to varnish the edges of naivety with ambition, to yearn for something more yet navigate on a razor's edge? Beneath the ruffles and lace of dresses worn at elite gatherings were souls laden with expectations and aspiration. Weishaupt was a man forged in contradictions—a dreamer who would become a conspirator, wielding hope while threading through shadows. It is a striking paradox: in his quest for enlightenment, he pushed forward into the very darkness he sought to illuminate.

As the Illuminati began to coalesce, the criteria for membership evolved into an enigmatic blend of intellect, social standing, and an unyielding proclivity for secrecy. This was a movement where paradoxes reveled in their contradictions—a sanctuary for those who wished to challenge the status quo while simultaneously securing their own. "Join us," Weishaupt implored, "and allow yourself to be the architect of a new destiny."

The recruitment of students and nobles didn't mirror the simplicity of a crusade. It was a nuanced dance that involved seduction, intrigue, and negotiation—each potential recruit a piece on a chessboard, and Weishaupt the cunning strategist. Every secret meeting, every whispered promise acted as powerful notes in a grand symphony composed not merely of rebellion, but of the hope and idealism that could ignite a revolution.

The tragic irony of this idealism was that it was inseparable from the very society they sought to critique. Beneath the surface of soaring aspirations, the layers of ambition could easily lead to dissolution. As nobility entertained students steeped in the agitation of revolutionary thought, it was apparent that the lines between loyalty and treachery blurry and ephemeral.

Time and again, history has shown that revolutions breed fractures where betrayals lie in wait, ever ready to pounce. Yet here, in these pivotal months of recruitment, a cohort began to form—a group bound not only by ideology but also by a shared destiny of ambition, exposure, and the relentless quest for something more. As they carved their ideals into the very fabric of society, an entire generation faced the inevitable question: would the tapestry they wove be one of enlightenment or, ultimately, a saga of collapse? The tension hung in the air as they considered their entry into a world far more intricate than any of them anticipated—one brewing with promise but aching with the weight of consequence.

Tactics of infiltration (Freemason lodges, clubs)

In the dusty corners of history, where light strains to penetrate the darkened recesses of human ambition, we find a meticulous web woven by the hands of the Illuminati. Beneath the polished surface of Enlightenment-era curiosity, factions formed and secrets thrived within the hallowed halls of Freemason lodges and clandestine clubs. This is where the true story of infiltration begins: a tale not just of dark alleys and whispered conspiracies but of intellectual prowess maneuvering through the corridors of power. Here, we will explore how a seemingly innocuous fraternity of stonemasons became a crucible for revolutionary thought and, ultimately, an unwitting breeding ground for subversive ideology.

As the 18th century dawned, Europe was undergoing unparalleled transformation—charismatic thinkers like Voltaire and Rousseau had set intellectual fires that illuminated the minds of the elite.

Eminent men convened under the auspices of Freemasonry, ostensibly for philanthropy and mutual improvement. But these lodges, often adorned with benevolent platitudes, cloaked an undercurrent of ambition. This revolution would not demand barricades but rather a subtle insurrection. The Illuminati saw the lodges not merely as meeting spaces, but as ideal platforms for infiltration—safe havens where revolutionary ideas could ferment without immediate detection.

Weishaupt's strategy was simple yet audacious. He recognized the utility of the Masonic network; it was vast, far-reaching, like the roots of an ancient oak. By embedding his followers within these lodges, the Illuminati could exploit their structures, engaging in an ideological battle where nuanced debate could mask the stakes. It was a masterstroke of socio-political chess, where each pawn was imbued with secret knowledge. The act of infiltration extended beyond mere membership; it involved understanding the motivating ethos of Masonry and appropriating its symbols, all while maintaining an air of genteel respectability.

Take, for example, the case of Johann Gottfried von Herder, a man whose intellectual curiosity drew him toward the shimmering façade of a Masonic lodge. Here he sought not only friendship, but a vehicle for his ideas. Yet, what lay beneath was a heated battleground where the ideals of freedom and enlightenment clashed, reshaping notions of identity and belonging. Herder ultimately became a conduit through which the Illuminati could circulate their radical tenets, using the spaces meant for brotherhood to foster revolutionary consciousness. While he believed he was creating a better world through dialogue, the Illuminati were carefully guiding conversations towards their own agenda—a gruesome irony neatly masked by the light of brotherhood.

But it wasn't just intellectuals who flocked to the lodges; they attracted the ambitious, the disenchanted, those seeking solace from the rigid hierarchies of the age. A lodge was a theater where the societal roles of the time—the church, monarchy, nobility—seemed malleable, at least momentarily. Beneath the chandeliers, an unholy symphony of ego and idealism played out. As the Illuminati sent forth its emissaries—whispered promises of enlightenment cloaked in secrecy—the lodges transformed into a breeding ground for radical ideology. Those who became their acolytes often found themselves besieged by the stark contrast between the Masonic embrace and the oppressive regimes that surveilled their every move.

As we traverse deeper into this labyrinth of infiltration, we encounter the ineffable allure of clandestine clubs. These intimate gatherings of disaffected thinkers formed their own networks, secret societies often birthed from the smoldering ashes of disillusionment. Each of these enclaves—often overlooked in the annals of history—became a microcosm for the revolutionary spirit. Where Freemasonry offered respectability, these clubs provided a sanctuary for the radical avant-garde, who sought nothing less than the dismantling of the old order.

One such gathering was the French Society of the Friends of the Revolution, a forum rife with fervor where thoughts flew like sparks in the air. Here, members engaged one another under the influence of wine and opulent chatter, their conversations morphing into rioting visions of a less restrained future. Among them was a clandestine cadre aligned with the Illuminati. Their intent was concealed beneath layers of camaraderie and philosophical discourse, yet their aim remained crystal clear: neither blind allegiance nor passivity would suffice. This was a groundswell rising, a current that would eventually sweep the old world away.

But the crux of infiltration lay not just in weaving oneself into the fabric of these organizations; it lay in the ability to emerge unscathed as the seams began to fray. This was no trivial pursuit; it required fortitude and finesse. Disguised as men of progress and decay, the Illuminati's representatives circulated the lodges and clubs, planting seeds of insurrection while portraying themselves as mere students of enlightenment. Yet, as their ideas spread, the atmosphere thickens with tension; each meeting becomes an electric charge of anticipation, a tightrope strung between friendship and treachery.

And there it is—the contrast so stark between aspiration and reality, between the celebrated ideals of brotherhood and the deep shadows of ambition. For every binding ritual performed in solemnity, for every toast raised to liberty, there existed an unvoiced question—at what cost would this revolution come? The lodges that once offered solace became treacherous grounds, where distinctions blurred beneath petty betrayals and incendiary whispers.

As the Illuminati grew emboldened, the very clubs and lodges that nurtured their ambitions became targets of scrutiny. The more they infiltrated, the more the light of suspicion turned back upon them. Elitist realms transformed into nightmarish shadows. What began as cunning tactics of infiltration soon morphed into a frenzied chase—a complex game of cat-and-mouse, with dogged authorities relentlessly pursuing the very ideals that once fueled revolutions. Here, ideology and reality collided in a profound irony; in the quest for enlightenment, the light grew dangerously dim.

In this chapter of infiltration, the Illuminati's ambition fueled an undeniable spiral toward collapse. As power amasses, it inevitably fractures, and we are left witnessing the tragic irony of revolutionary zeal morphing into desperate entanglements. The glittering façade of these lodges and clubs obscured their true potential—a ticking time bomb, ready to erupt once the delicate balance was disturbed. What emerges is a narrative of profound reflection: the struggle for meaningful change often leaves chaos in its wake, and sometimes the darkest ambitions cloak themselves in the noblest intentions.

Growth across Bavaria

At the turn of the 1770s, Bavaria was a crucible of thought, a tangled web where ideas collided with age-old traditions, and ambition meandered through cobbled streets like the Isar River itself. Under the waning influence of clerical power, educated elites began to coalesce around a common cause. They were searching—not merely for enlightenment, but for a revolution of the mind. Here in this lush landscape, dotted with Baroque castles and verdant fields, a clandestine movement was stirring, nourished by the fertile ground of intellectual inquiry and the poison of an oppressive regime.

Adam Weishaupt, a name not yet etched in the annals of history but on the verge of igniting an inferno of ideology, was at the helm of this burgeoning insurgence. As a professor at the University of Ingolstadt, he stood at the crossroads of enlightenment and fanaticism, of liberation and tyranny. Beneath the polished surface of academia lay the very real threat of censorship and repression—a gentility paid for in obedience and silence. Weishaupt's vision? To challenge this stifling orthodoxy, to uproot the age-old shackles of superstition with intellectual clarity.

The Illuminati began, not with the grandeur of conspirators in dark rooms, but with whispered meetings held in candle-lit corners. Weishaupt's earliest recruits were not the wealthy elites, but rather the fervent, hungry young minds—the inquisitive students who dared to reach beyond their textbooks. Together, they forged a bond carved from shared ideals: reason over dogma, autonomy over allegiance, and knowledge as the ultimate path to liberation. How intoxicating it must have felt to dream of a society unfettered by the church's grip and the aristocracy's scorn.

Yet, as the movement gained traction, the implications of this intellectual awakening became starkly apparent. The goal was never merely to critique the status quo but to dismantle it piece by piece. Would these young radicals even begin to grasp the weight of their ambitions? Beneath their fervent discourse and scholarly allegiance lay the seeds of conflict—an ideological divergence from the serene respectability of Bavarian society. As the sun set over Augsburg, casting long shadows of the Gothic spires, the storm clouds of dissent began to gather.

Weishaupt's ambitions grew in tandem with his network. Fraternal ties were formed amidst the backdrop of a society clinging desperately to tradition. The first iteration of the Order was founded in 1776—an irony that wouldn't escape a nation wrestling with its own identity. As their membership expanded, the Illuminati encroached upon the very fabric of Bavarian life. Yet, the genius of Weishaupt lay in his recognizing that raw ambition had to be tempered by discretion. The society operated like a clandestine river, carving unseen paths through the heart of Bavaria, rumbling quietly beneath the noise of the surface world.

As branches spread out from Bavaria to embrace neighboring territories, their influence began to ripple outward. They weren't just recruiting future leaders, but also securing liaisons with Freemasons, another semi-secret society forged from the anvils of Enlightenment thought. The Illuminati thrived on collaborative ambition—a deceptive melding where visions intertwined and the thirst for knowledge morphed into a brotherhood beset with the irresistible desire for power. Before it all unraveled, they saw themselves not just as harbingers of change, but as architects of a new world order, conceptualizing doctrines that sought to anchor politicians, thinkers, and even the disillusioned common man.

Take, for instance, the clandestine meeting in the summer of 1779—the scent of musty tomes permeated the air while lantern-light flickered against cold stone walls. It was here that they unfolded the doctrine of Enlightenment: equality, liberty, fraternity. Such lofty ideals cloaked in powerful rhetoric that inspired like an elixir. They imagined a society where rulers would bow to reason, not bloodlines; where justice would outshine favoritism. The allure rested in this intoxicating vision of humanity freed from the tyrannies that had shackled it for centuries.

What remains of those cavernous debates lingered in whispers, making their way to the ears of secret-police informants and jealous rivals alike. As Bavaria trembled with the heartbeat of ambition, danger was a constant specter lurking just beyond the candlelight—an inescapable truth that tempered every triumph with fear. The inquisitors lingered, their eyes searching for heresy, their hands itching to quench subversion. Weishaupt recognized that the mantle of greatness was fraught; every expansion brought threats navigating the narrow waters between courage and folly.

As the Illuminati sought to propagate its ideas, their philosophy morphed into something more than dialogue. It seeped into the cultural fabric, infusing art, literature, and discourse with a hitherto unseen vigor. But here lies the eternal paradox—while they ought to have flourished as harbingers of reason, their very desire for influence birthed suspicion. Ambition whetted its bewitching edge; the minds ignited by dream soon found themselves threading between the traps laid by their own aspirations.

Could the very ideals that bound them also be their undoing? The scheme grew tangled as new recruits entered the fold, and with them, fresh ambitions and aspirations arose. There was a palpable tension between the original vision Weishaupt espoused and the elusive nature of collective power. How could they galvanize their fellow thinkers while remaining invisible, yet impactful? This paradox simmered just beneath the veneer of revolutionary zeal.

As the decade wore on, Bavarian society began to take note, its elite sharpening their criticism, arming themselves with old proclamations of loyalty. Weishaupt's attempts to orchestrate a revolution through education were viewed with equal parts fascination and disdain. Ordinary folk remained unaware, shifting beneath the weight of mundane life, while the hidden elite debated the virtues and vices of the emerging order.

In this landscape of burgeoning ambition, as Bavaria smoldered with prophetic fervor, history would soon demand answers. Before it all unraveled, one crucial question lay dormant among hidden ambitions and dazzling illusions: could they ascend into greatness without courting disaster, or would their dreams devour them whole? Beneath the shroud of hope, the real battleground remained the hearts and minds of the populace—an invisible war that churned relentlessly beneath the surface, waiting to be unleashed with the power of an unyielding tide.

Chapter 4: Conflict and Exposure

Tensions with Freemasons

Beneath the polished surface of enlightenment and brotherhood in the 18th century, a tempest raged—ideological warfare cloaked in the genteel garments of fellowship. As the Illuminati emerged, fueled by the audacity of reason against the backdrop of a deteriorating European order, they found themselves straddling the fault line of conflict with the Freemasons, a fraternity that had long wielded both influence and secrecy, drawing a dichotomy between its venerable traditions and the radical reformist zeal of Weishaupt's creation.

The roots of Freemasonry ran deep into the soil of European society, nourished by a mixture of mystique and mischief. For generations, its lodges had drawn together men of distinction who sought not only camaraderie but a sanctuary from the capricious winds of political upheaval. They were an amalgamation of merchants, artisans, and the occasional nobleman, hidden behind the worn doors of their temples, engaged in rituals where symbols spoke louder than words. Yet the very essence of their society—its inherent exclusivity—would soon provoke the ire of new revolutionaries spurred by the spirit of radical Enlightenment.

At a cursory glance, the Illuminati and Freemasons appeared aligned in their quest for freedom and rational thought. But as their paths converged, it became increasingly clear that the stark contrasts in philosophy and method placed them on a collision course. Where Freemasons preached the virtues of gradual reform, the Illuminati advocated for revolution—a reconfiguration of societal hierarchies that challenged not only monarchs but the very fabric of established societies. Weishaupt's order sought a theoretical underpinning of ultimate equality; the Masons, with their carefully constructed hierarchies, represented a far more complex tapestry of social stratification.

The conflict simmered like a pot nearing the boil. It was in the city of Munich, in the very heart of Bavaria, that the tension first manifested between these two clandestine organizations. The Illuminati sought to infiltrate Masonic lodges, viewing the brotherhood as a vital target for recruitment, hopeful that their existing networks of power could be transformed into instruments of their revolutionary goals. But they naïvely underestimated the deeply entrenched Masonic ethos. The Freemasons, who cherished their hard-won autonomy and ritualistic traditions, saw the Illuminati as interlopers, uninvited guests looking to disrupt their carefully curated banquet of influence.

With every clandestine meeting, the rift widened. Weishaupt, ever the strategist, attempted to undermine the Masonic hegemony through subversion. His rhetoric painted the Masons as complacent relics of an old order, trapped in the chains of their own privilege. They were, in his eyes, men afraid of the fire that he was all too eager to stoke. In turn, Masonic leaders, feeling the creeping threat of anarchy, rallied to protect their reputation and preserve their lodges' integrity, launching a campaign to expose what they considered the nefarious aspirations of the Illuminati—actions that, paradoxically, only served to weave the two factions closer together in an intricate dance of cat and mouse.

Let us pause for a moment to reflect: what drove men to the shadows, to lurk within the dimly lit corners of society, debating liberty while the rustle of revolution echoed just outside their door? There was something hauntingly intoxicating about the prospect of unchecked power; it entranced both dreamers and doomsayers alike. As the Illuminati took bold steps to unveil the mechanisms of manipulation, they often wielded their own propensity for secrecy, veiling their true ambitions under layers of philosophical posturing—an irony that seldom slipped their notice.

As the tension escalated, the fabric of society began to fray. The political landscape of Bavaria, and indeed Europe itself, surged and churned, reminiscent of a brewing storm. Freemasonry's roots in established authority offered momentary respite, while the Illuminati's radical philosophies flickered like wild flames yearning for oxygen. Common ground eluded them, and soon they found themselves embroiled in skirmishes not just in the ether of ideology, but in real, tangible confrontations.

The writing was on the wall by the late 1780s, as both organizations jockeyed for influence against the backdrop of the French Revolution's unfolding chaos. The remnants of royal power were under siege, and with it, the Masons, too, felt their position threatened. Rumors and whispers flowed through the taverns and salons of leading cities, blurring the line between reality and hysteria. The Illuminati, already painted as the villain in a growing conspiracy narrative, straddled the limits of acceptability, while the Masonic lodges clung to their traditions, desperate to preserve some semblance of order amidst the swirling panic.

Casting the net yet wider, both organizations began embroiling themselves in a battle for public perception. The Illuminati fabricated incriminating letters, insinuating the Masons' collusion with the old order, while Mason dissidents took to pamphlets and whispers to expose the subversive plots of Weishaupt's cohorts. Each faction issued a clarion call to its followers, animating the rhetoric of college debates, salon discussions, and secret meetings with vivid accusations and elaborate counterclaims. There's a distinct thrill when tension transforms into outright conflict, igniting imaginations even as it fractures lives.

Then, like a shattering glass, the tension exploded in 1785 with a swift clampdown from the Bavarian authorities. Outrageously dramatic—perhaps theater itself—Louis IV's decree against the Illuminati felt like the desperate gasp of a dying regime, fearing revolution's caustic tide. The Illuminati had become a scapegoat for deeper societal ills, transforming the once-alluring idea of equality into a sinister caricature. As the noose of oppression tightened around them, they found themselves forced into the shadows, their every move monitored, ridiculed, if not outright feared.

Before it all unraveled, it was clear: the tensions between the Illuminati and Freemasons served not just as an emblem of two dissonant philosophies but as a reflection of the larger chaos engulfing society. For every brother who raised a glass to toast liberty in a Masonic lodge, another clandestine figure plotted the shifts of power from the shadows beneath the surface. The stage was set, but history remained stubbornly unpredictable, often driven by the eager ambitions of men unwilling to recognize the folly they sowed in the name of revolution.

And so, the world witnessed the crashing together of lightning and soil—two factions, each convinced their ideals would birth a new dawn, caught in the dizzying whirl of ideology and reality. The tension wasn't merely a footnote; it was a vortex that pulled lives into its depths, each chosen path unraveling the lives connected to the tightly woven social fabric of their age.

Clerical opposition and spies

In an age that savored enlightenment like the finest wine, the Illuminati's ideology bubbled beneath the polished surface of Bavarian prairies. Their ambition, cloaked in the guise of reason and fraternity, was ballooning towards an insatiable desire for dominance over the mind. Yet, as we dive deeper into Chapter 4, it becomes glaringly evident that all revolutions attract their share of opposition. Clerical opposition to the Illuminati was not merely an act of resistance; it formed a cauldron of fear, paranoia, and intricate espionage that ultimately laid bare the darker corners of a movement striving for illumination.

The clergy, guardians of divine order, found themselves ensnared in a landscape growing increasingly populated by revolutionary ideas. Their dominion was threatened not just ideologically, but existentially. Amidst the caffeine-fueled discussions in coffeehouses, curveballs thrown by freethinkers like Weishaupt were challenging the moral fabric long woven into the German Empire. It was here that the clergy veered sharply from passive concern to active opposition—a shift that manifested in unexpected and often explosive ways.

In a rare moment of vulnerability, one cleric wrote of the "foul play" lurking behind the noble banner of Enlightenment. Fear flared, ignited by whispers that followers of the Illuminati espoused doctrines encouraging skepticism towards religious authority. To the clergy, this was not merely an intellectual scrutiny—it was a direct assault on faith itself. They painted these insurgents with sinister brushstrokes, portraying them as demons masquerading in scholarly garb, intent on uprooting societal norms. It was not just the church that felt the quakes; society's nerves became frayed at the notion that eternal truths could be comic fodder in this carnival of rationalism.

As dissent simmered, clergy began joining hands with the various factions that formed a response to this insurrection in ideas. From the pulpit, the illuminators were branded as threat and villain, tied inextricably to the broader fears of revolution that rattled Europe like a fevered nightmare. The suspicion of collusion grew, and every new idea was examined under a magnifying glass of hysteria—were the Illuminati secretly plotting a coup against God's chosen order?

The standard-bearers of faith were not alone in their fears; their efforts were bolstered by a cadre of spies and informants. The underbelly of society stirred with clandestine activity, and the shadowy figure of the informant became both a savior and a harbinger of chaos. It was a toxic alliance formed by the clergy and the state, both craving stabilities so badly that they emboldened each other in their shared suspicion. To counter the enigmatic threat of the Illuminati, they cultivated a network of informants who fed their insatiable appetite for knowledge about the movement's inner workings.

This was not merely espionage; it was a calculated gamble. The clergy recognized the necessity of maintaining a façade of control amidst their burning anxieties. They tapped into the growing tension between governing powers and revolutionary thinkers, acting as both rat and sedative to the gnawing fear that a new order was elbowing its way into existence. These individuals, entrenched with sects and lodges, became trustworthy spies—marked not by loyalty, but by the desperation of the contentions swirling around them.

Some infiltrators, despite their intentions, found themselves deeply enmeshed in the labyrinth of Illuminati thought. A schoolteacher, once dragged into the fray by their well-intentioned but reckless quest for knowledge, became embroiled in a series of dialogues and secret meetings that took him into the heart of dissent. The abrupt contrasts of enlightenment philosophy, and dogma collided violently, leaving scars that told tales of transformation. In the aftermath, these spies, too, bore the weight of conflicting ideologies—their lives straddling the line between advancement and betrayal.

Yet, considered from another angle, this dialectic did not merely fortify the clergy's resolve. Paranoia began to permeate the church's very framework, gnawing at corners where faith should have stood unyielding. This frenzy suggested an ironic truth: the weapons wielded in the name of divine order and societal preservation often became their own undoing. The more power the church sought to consolidate in the face of this intellectual upheaval, the more it revealed its own fragility.

The innovation of espionage led the clergy to engage in some curious practices. Gathering intel suddenly became ritualistic. They developed codes, a spycraft amalgamation of cryptography and biblical references, shuffling secret messages between parishes under the guise of sermon notes. A tension-filled page, with faint notes slid behind the altar, captured the mood of the time, one where cross-wires could spark inter-faction strife. With every ounce of deceptive rhetoric, the clergy morphed into fearful predators, unable to curtail the flow of ideas surging around them.

It is here we witness the maw of conflict open wider. In one gripping duel of clandestine meetings, a priest eyeing an Illuminati member across the table felt the weight of absolution suspended like a fragile glass ornament above his head. In the battle of hearts and minds, this slim volume tossed between them—the Bible's questionable interpretations laid bare for juxtaposition—revealed a profound desperation that bubbled beneath the orthodoxy. The resonant echoes of ideas, cultural yearning, and spiritual condemnation led to paranoia that curdled into betrayal.

Yet, the constant tension brought about a schism within the society that sought to uphold the old ways. Employees turned informants turned doubters—long tables host to clandestine meetings spun webs of discontent. It was a heavy play, and just as the spies wielded whispered truths like daggers, the rift turned personal, splitting loyalties and shattering the veneer of camaraderie.

As the intricacies of clerical opposition spiraled into an unrelenting storm of suspicion, one thing remained clear: the paranoia ramified into something greater, a relentless tide that inexorably shaped both the clergy's identity and their perception of the already fractious movements of their time. The delicate threads of trust unraveled, leaving behind a legacy of shadows and whispers that would haunt the church long after the last candle had flickered out. To face the Illuminati meant confronting an ideology that symbolized the quintessential struggle between old orders and transformative thought. Beneath the polished surface of history, real conflict erupted—a war fought not in the open, but beneath the surface of society's consciousness, where illumination and chaos danced their perilous tango.

Internal debates and betrayals

Beneath the polished surface of convivial gathering and cerebral pursuits, the inner workings of the Bavarian Illuminati revealed an unsettling chaos—an intellectual quagmire riddled with conflicting ideologies, secret ambitions, and personal betrayals. As the light of reason flickered in candlelit chambers, figures who once shared a common vision began exhibiting the very traits they sought to eradicate in society: envy, ambition, and the ruthless quest for power. This was the ground where enlightenment met its antithesis, and the seeds of conflict took root.

Adam Weishaupt, the movement's architect, had envisioned a fraternity steeped in philosophical rigor—a bastion against the encroaching darkness of dogma and ignorance. Yet, as the society grew, so too did its ambitions and the fractures within. Members of the Illuminati, drawn from the powerful echelons of society, found that their allegiances were as fleeting as the ideas they professed. Among them were scholars, clerics, nobles, and fervent revolutionaries, each bearing their own agenda, each lingering specter of discontent lurking beneath the minuscule layers of fraternity.

Take Christian Fürchtegott Gellert, the famed poet whose eloquence charmed many a mind. He was initially swept into the movement by its utopian promise, but as discussions morphed into machinations, Gellert grew increasingly uneasy. The bright visions of enlightenment began to sour, sounding discordant notes that played like a lone violin out of tune. Gellert, feeling trapped in a web spun by lofty ideals, experienced an epiphany: the Illuminati's raison d'être had blurred into a canvas of insatiable ambition. Discussions soon evolved from lofty philosophical debates to strategic plots cloaked in secrecy, reminiscent of the very tyranny they sought to dismantle. There was something dangerously intoxicating about the power of secrets—a promise of autonomy twinned with an implicit threat of betrayal.

The temptation for supremacy ignited a power struggle among the members. The tale of Johann Heinrich Gottlieb von Justi serves as a sobering reminder of this internal strife. A brilliant economic theorist, von Justi epitomized the clash of ideals within the society. He was a fervent advocate for free thought but found himself increasingly at odds with Weishaupt's authoritative governance. Discontent simmered as von Justi wrestled with the growing realization that the warm embrace of camaraderie had begun to suffocate the innovative spirit of their cause. His writings called for a more democratic approach, yet it was this very defiance that made him enemies. As whispers of his dissent circulated, a deadly game of chess emerged in which he became both pawn and king, ultimately laying the groundwork for his own ostracism.

Amidst these factions, betrayal roared like a fierce wind, scattering alliances like autumn leaves. The shadow of dissolution grew heavy, suffocating the noble aspirations harbored within the organization. Weishaupt, once a visionary revered for his intellect, now faced the ultimate test: could an ideology rooted in credo foster its own destruction? The possibility lingered in the air, thickening with every clandestine meeting held in smoky taverns and hidden chambers.

Members exchanged not only ideas but also glances laced with suspicion—the age-old fear of assassination lurking just beneath smiles forced onto weary faces.

Enter the formidable figure of Baron Adolf von Knigge. Initially, he infused the Illuminati with momentum, championing the cause of social reform and expanding its reach. But beneath his charisma lurked the instincts of a cunning strategist. As he consolidated authority, his actions sowed discord, and the fractioning began. An argument triggered by a supposedly harmless debate erupted into a full-blown confrontation. Accusations erupted like flames, each interjector stoking the fires of enmity, revealing thinly veiled agendas. The debate devolved quickly into a vicious free-for-all, personal aspirations and grudges laid bare for all to witness. Von Knigge, moving nimbly in the chaos, seemed to relish the discord. He maneuvered others like puppets on strings, preying upon their weaknesses to further entrench his own power.

Conflict became the soil in which ideas began to rot. The very bonds that had united the members soon frayed, unraveling the fabric of their collective vision. Voices once eager to challenge the status quo became insidious whispers of discontent. "What is the point of liberation," they questioned, "if we cannot liberate ourselves from one another?" A disturbing irony began to unfurl: the minds that sought to unify under the banner of reason found their collective strength weakening as resentments pooled beneath the surface.

Simultaneously, external forces compounded their internal strife. The German government, wary of the burgeoning power of the Illuminati, began laying its own traps. In response to rumors that swirled around the society like vultures around carrion, the authorities cultivated a narrative that depicted the organization as a breeding ground for subversion. Their orchestrated campaigns played on the fractures already present, whispering allegations of conspiracies, treason, and treachery that infiltrated the very existence of the Illuminati. Friends became foes on an amplified stage soaked in public suspicion.

Before it all unraveled, the Illuminati was caught in a web woven from ambition, ideology, and betrayal—an interplay so intricate that even its own members struggled to comprehend the extent of their collective destiny. It is a tale that echoes through the ages, a reminder that even the grandest of visions can collapse under the weight of internal conflicts. Just as the protagonists of an epic would stumble in the throes of passion, these illuminated souls wrestled with their own humanity: brilliant yet deeply flawed, eager yet devoured by ambition. With every betrayal, every simmering discord, they painted a stark reminder that the revolution is not merely born in the fires of change; it can also be extinguished by the very hands that crafted it.

Chapter 5: Suppression and Fall

The government crackdown of 1785

The year 1785 marks a pivotal juncture in the fraught history of the Illuminati, where the specter of state power coalesced into a deliberate, almost surgical strike against the burgeoning network of revolutionary thought. As the Fourth Estate began to be an uneasy partner in the realm of ideas, Bavaria witnessed the rise of an insidious panic among its rulers. Beneath the polished surface of enlightenment ideals lay an undercurrent of fear; that which might liberate the mind could also ignite insurrection.

On the cusp of a new era, the very existence of Weishaupt's order, with its tenets echoing through secret meetings and hushed conversations, posed an unsettling challenge to the status quo. In a nation where loyalty to the crown was sacrosanct, the menace was not merely theoretical; it was a challenge to the established order itself. In 1785, the Bavarian government, spurred by mounting apprehensions, embarked on a crackdown that would reverberate through the annals of history.

At the center of this maelstrom was the Grand Duke of Bavaria, Karl Theodor, a ruler whose aversion to the fraying threads of authority intensified following the insurrectionary fervor sweeping across Europe. The middle classes, once complacent in their obedience, began to stir with aspirations towards personal liberties, emboldened by the fiery rhetoric of revolutionaries across the Atlantic. What was considered a harmless society, one that sought enlightenment and reason, became labeled as a harbinger of chaos. Within weeks, the secretive meetings that fostered intellectual camaraderie would, in an ironic twist, be declared treasonous.

The government's response was brutal in its efficiency, characterized by a mixture of cunning and clumsiness that only served to expose the raw nerves of an empire on the brink. Secret police infiltrated meetings, keystroke artists scribed the ideological ruminations of the Illuminati with an urgency bordering on paranoia, while pamphlets condemning the organization circulated with the vigor of wildfire. For the first time in their short existence, the members of the Illuminati stood as targets—the hunted rather than the hunters they had envisioned.

Symbolic of this tumult was the arrest of prominent members like theologian Johann Gottlieb Fichte, whose ideals had flirted with the edges of both philosophy and insurrection. The backlash was swift and merciless. One fateful evening, a group of five Illuminati members found themselves encircled in the very heart of their subversive gatherings—captured in an act as spontaneous and elementary as a game of chess suddenly interrupted by a marauding eagle. Fear ran rampant as they were led away, their fates intertwined with the repressive machinery of the state.

Yet in the midst of this crackdown, a curious phenomenon began to unfold. Many former members, their backs pressed against the grim wall of authority, began to reappraise their choices—confessing that their allegiances had been rooted as much in personal ambition as the heady ideals of Enlightenment thought. Those who had once exulted in the Illuminati's mission now hastily distanced themselves, like rats abandoning a sinking ship, seeking absolution in the very doctrines that they had once sought to dismantle.

Fiction writ large; what had begun as an avatar of change was now a paradox, representing both the best and the worst of human ambition. Membership dwindled under the heavy weight of scrutiny, the ideals of brotherhood fading into a ghostly echo. Weishaupt, who had once envisioned a society of thinkers unfettered by the shackles of dogma, now found himself displaced within the very movement he had engineered.

The controversies and anxieties surrounding the Illuminati reached their zenith, permeating the public consciousness. In small towns, taverns, and salons, whispers of conspiracy swirled like smoke from a dying fire. Here, amidst the low hum of trepidation, the arrest and turmoil of the Illuminati became fodder for intrigue, simmering beneath the surface of Bavarian society. As the regime tightened its grip, the image of the Illuminati metamorphosed from mere theorists to boogeymen, inflating the significance of the lives of men whose aspirations had never been more substantial than free debate and radical enlightenment.

Weishaupt, now a fugitive amidst the storm he had unwittingly unleashed, did not capitulate to despair. Instead, he retreated into the shadows of his ideals, penning missives that lamented the shortcomings of his followers—writings that would unveil the fissures between ideological purity and human frailty. It was here, in the written word, that the seeds of resistance were sown, a testament to the enduring conflict between the state's ambition and the individual's desire for liberty.

For the ruling elite, this suppression came more than a decade after their ascension into an age characterized by the rhetoric of freedom and reason. The notion of dissent, once reviled as mere treason, became ennobled by the notion of sacrifice for a broader cause. But as history would show, the state's persecution of the Illuminati was as much an admission of fear as it was an assertion of power—a clumsy attempt to reign in the forces of thought that were spiraling out of their control.

As the walls closed in around the order, the ramifications shone light on an essential truth: revolutions do not die quietly. In their death throes, they breathe new life into ideas, sparking movements that could never have been anticipated. Those who believed they could snuff out the light of inquiry instead found themselves illuminating the dark corners of a human spirit intent on manifesting its identity. Before the dust settled on the streets of Munich, the effects of 1785 would precipitate a reexamination of revolutions across Europe, each inching closer towards ideals that could no longer be muffled.

What lay ahead for the Illuminati became a landscape marked by irony. The government crackdown was not merely a moment of enforced silence but a catalyst for transformative thought. Their suppression birthed a dichotomy that paralleled the lives of men like Weishaupt, who believed they could out-think tyranny, only to be engulfed by it. Even in turmoil, the struggle for enlightenment continued to pulse—with every arrest, every hastily forgotten debate, resonating through the annals of civilization's fight for reason.

Ultimately, the showdown of 1785 served as an unwelcome reminder that those who trade freedom for stability rarely realize what is lost until it is irretrievably gone. It foreshadowed the unraveling of not just a clandestine society but revealed the fragility of progress itself—

a precarious balance that remains at the core of our understanding of both revolution and reality.

Arrests, trials, and exiles

As the sun began to set in the 18th century, a shadow loomed larger than the collective ambitions of secret societies. With each passing year, the energy of Enlightenment thought stewed beneath the surface of Europe, simmering with the visions of liberty and reason. Yet the thin veneer of progress belied an undercurrent of fear—fear of dissent, fear of subversion. And at the center of this brewing storm stood the Illuminati, a small band of idealists caught in the crosshairs of a society unwilling to accept their radical views.

By the 1780s, the once-esoteric meetings of Weishaupt's group had drawn the unwanted attention of sovereign powers. The Bavarian government, gripped by paranoia, began its hunt for scapegoats to quell the rising tumult. But the Illuminati had initially been an intellectual refuge. The pursuit of knowledge, a potpourri of philosophy, and shared aspirations flourished in candle-lit rooms, yet now those same spaces became a trap. Preachers of enlightenment soon found themselves tarred as purveyors of chaos.

In May 1784, the government announced an edict against the Illuminati, branding them a clandestine threat. What's intriguing here is not merely the decree itself, which could have faded into the annals of ignored legislation, but rather the ripples it sent through society. Trust unraveled. Friends turned on each other, eager to exonerate themselves from the looming specter of suspicion. Beneath the polished surface of camaraderie, paranoia festered.

By the fall of that year, the arrests began—an avalanche of detentions that would ripple through the Bavarian countryside. A network forged in loyalty became a crucible of betrayal. Among the first to fall was Johann Gottlieb Fichte, an intellectual who had once found solace in the writings of his Illuminati brethren. Known for his staunch defense of freedom, Fichte suddenly found his philosophical torch extinguished in the shadow of accusations. What had been a community of like-minded thinkers had now transformed into a field of landmines where one misstep could lead to a devastating explosion of consequence.

Witnessing the arrests instilled an eerie silence in the hearts of those who had not been taken. Friends would return from meetings with vacant expressions, the innate vibrancy of their beliefs snuffed out. Beneath the surface of frustration and fear, a visceral question hung in the air—had their visions been naïve? Were they criminal heirs to a philosophy that could only be crushed beneath the heel of tyrants?

Public trials soon followed the arrests, acting as both spectacle and warning. The once-private criticisms of tyranny transformed into a stage for the authorities to demonstrate their power. Onlookers filled the benches, eager for the drama that unfolded as the bribed, the coerced, and the passionate took to the stand, either to condemn their former comrades or to defend an ideal that seemed to dissolve like mist. The law, once seen as an arbiter of justice, now wielded a scorched-earth policy against dissent.

Weishaupt himself—while not yet arrested—was relegated to the shadows, a puppet master who had lost control of his marionettes. The irony lay thick: as the architect of a vision meant to elevate humanity through reason, he now faced a future where reason had forsaken him. Clandestine gatherings turned into frantic whispers, discussions morphing into fevered attempts to preserve what little remained of their society. They spoke in hushed tones of “exile,” a word infused with both despair and opportunity. To escape persecution might also mean the end of everything they fought for.

In an abrupt twist of fate, in 1785, Weishaupt was summoned before the very authorities he had sought to enlighten. While many of his followers clung to the vestiges of hope that he would emerge unscathed, the outcome was all but predetermined. The atmosphere felt charged, as if the room itself inhaled, collectively anticipating the fall of a man who had dared to challenge an iron grip.

When the verdict came, it resonated with the finality of a funeral bell clasping the broken promises of the Enlightenment. Weishaupt was exiled, stripped of his privileges, and thrust into a life of obscurity. The tension between ambition and reality collapsed upon itself, with Weishaupt finding solitude in a foreign land—an irony so bitter one could almost taste it. Ironically, the exile brought forth a mix of relief and dread; as he departed, he wondered if the philosophical society he built would crumble in his absence.

But it wasn’t merely the expulsion of Weishaupt that struck at the heart of the Illuminati’s endurance. It was the exodus of hope that flowed through the veins of the members left scattered across Europe. Like leaves in a storm, each carried away both remnants of original intent and the emotional bruises of defeat. In the wake of tyrannical suppression, many a once-vibrant revolutionary spirit found solace in blending back into the very fabric of society they had sought to reform.

The tension escalated and plummeted, contorting lives and societies in its grasp. It was a curious paradox: through their suppression, the Illuminati made history's footnote—a shadowy whisper rather than a declared roar. Each exile bore a legacy of disillusionment, marred by cracked ideals, but ignited flickers that would inspire future generations to pick up the threads.

In those final trials of men who dreamed too boldly, we're left with a lingering question. What does it mean to fight for truth in a world that deems it a threat? The men of Weishaupt's vision may have been cast into the underbelly of society, but their conviction, however fractured, remained dormant beneath the surface. It awaited the moment when gallant notions of democracy and liberty could emerge again from their shroud, ready to be reborn—prepared to confront the very ideologies that had conspired against them.

The Illuminati had begun as a rebellion of thought but morphed into a cautionary tale of ambition undone. As we probe deeper into their fall, we join them on their journey—not merely as historians but as seekers of truth—a truth, they believed, would one day be central to humanity's salvation—even if at great cost. As we turn the page, we stand on the brink of a resistant legacy that, even when shattered, leaves us pondering: What happens when ideology confronts stark reality? The answer lies in shadows yet to be illuminated.

The disappearance of the order

In the late summer months of 1786, the currents of power began to turn against a seemingly innocuous fraternity cloaked in the writings of truth and enlightenment. The Bavarian Illuminati, birthed in the shadows of university lecture halls, was marked for extinction by forces that thrived in obscurity and intimidation. Beneath the polished surface of intellectual discourse ran the serpentine underbelly of political paranoia—with fear and suspicion rising in equal measure. The Order, once a beacon of reason and progressive ideals, found itself ensnared in a net woven from whispers and volatile ideology.

Their expulsion from public life was nothing short of dramatic, a sweeping tide that threatened to erase them from history's ledger. The accusations fell like daggers against the fabric of society: subversion, sedition, and conspiracy all laced with the fuel of societal hysteria. Those who once gathered in candle-lit rooms to discuss philosophy and the betterment of human society now faced the unyielding hammer of authority. What had begun as a scholarly group dedicated to reason transformed into a scapegoat for the insecurities of a ruling class desperate to cling to the status quo.

The catalyst for this transformation can be traced to the ruling elites of Bavaria, a coalition of church officials and political leaders who viewed the Illuminati as a direct challenge to their age-old prerogatives. In 1784, a royal edict sought to terminate the Order's activities, labeling them a secret society bent on the overthrow of established religious and political institutions. What, on closer inspection, may have appeared as an earnest endeavor to foster enlightenment among the populace became unjustly conflated with charges of rebellion, cloaked in the paranoia that history often provokes.

Just as the dim light of reason had flickered into a flame of revolt, it quickly began to dwindle under the weight of mounting suppression. Yet, amid the chaos, one cannot ignore the fascinating irony—the very conditions that led to the suppression of the Illuminati also highlighted the significant social changes sweeping across Europe. During this period, the Enlightenment's ideals seeped into the public consciousness, drawing sharp lines of contrast between the fervent thirst for knowledge and the iron chains of tradition. In the minds of the ruling class, the source of such fervor was not the propagation of thought, but rather a conspiracy to topple their reign.

Before it all unraveled, Weishaupt and his fellow Illuminati had sought to operate within the boundaries of societal norms while altering them from within. Their meetings held the promise of transformation, a notion that uplifted the common man against the reigning dogmas. And yet, as their doctrines spread through influence and intellectual engagement, the fear of an insurrection loomed ever larger among those entrenched in power. A movement based on reason was marked for extermination—a tragic irony for a society desperate for rationalist thought.

In the autumn of 1786, alarm bells resounded as law enforcement agents raided clandestine meetings, disrupting discussions and scattering scholars like quail before a hawk. Personal correspondences were seized, manuscripts confiscated, and members imprisoned, forced into silence under the ever-watchful eye of a state emboldened by fear. The dissipation of the Illuminati was as swift as it was ruthless; their impact, however, could not be relegated to the annals of anonymity. The ghost of their ambition lingered still, haunting the corridors of power with whispered truths that could not so easily be exorcized.

The case of Adam Weishaupt himself is illustrative of this unnerving irony. Once a celebrated professor, he was reduced to an exile, a man reviled by the very institutions he had strived to enlighten. Bereft of his followers and stripped of credibility, Weishaupt sought refuge across borders, pondering the irony of his situation. Was it possible that reason could be extinguished by fear? Could the light of enlightenment ultimately be snuffed out by the very darkness it sought to illuminate? Faces once illuminated by burgeoning ideas turned towards shadows, contemplating the fate of an order that had striven to carve a new path for humanity.

Historians often overlook these weary travelers—the clandestine thinkers and those passionate crusaders who dared to dream in a time when dissent was silenced. In their disappearance lies a significant story, woven into the fabric of revolutionary fervor that marked Europe's turn toward rebellion. As political upheaval sparked from France to America, their philosophy silently crept into the minds of those who dared to resist authority, manifesting in unforeseen ways: through pamphlets, publications, and whispered commands shifted across borders.

For the Illuminati, the tightening noose of suppression also exposed the fractured alliances within their ranks, setting the stage for a schism. Not all who claimed allegiance to Weishaupt shared his vision for social transformation, and divisions emerged among factions, each clutching their own burgeoning ideologies. It was a microcosm of revolution: the clash between idealism and pragmatism, theory and practice, unfolding at the threshold of philosophical undoing.

As these complexities unfolded, it became evident that the dissolution of the order did not herald its end. On the contrary, the themes of freedom and rationality they had propagated continued to resonate, echoing across the tenets of burgeoning revolutionary movements. History has a way of bending around oppression, finding ways to surface amid turmoil like roots breaking through pavement.

The disappearance of the Illuminati preceded grander confrontations over political power and societal structure. Their fate did not solely belong to their actions in darkened rooms; it was enmeshed in the very fabric of the Enlightenment, a removed story crystallizing within every insurrection that followed. Thus, while we may conclude the chapter of their official existence, we merely scratch the surface of a broader narrative—one that questions the persistence of ideas long after their progenitors have vanished into obscurity.

Indeed, the spirit of revolution does not die; it morphs, survives, and re-emerges like a phoenix from its ashes. As the outlines of history shimmer beneath the chaos, the shadow of the Illuminati reveals itself—not as an aberration of reason, but rather as the first pulse of a radical future waiting to be born.

Chapter 6: Afterlives in Print and Myth

Pamphlets and polemics in the French Revolution

In the fevered cauldron of revolutionary France, where the echoes of the Bastille crumbled the old order and liberated radical ideas, pamphlets became the lifeblood of a nascent public sphere. They were the hand grenades of ideology, mercilessly tossed into the heart of a tumultuous society, and the sheer volume of these written provocations would overwhelm the confines of any library. Nestled among the pamphlets of sensationalists and republicans were the whispers of clandestine societies, their ideas crafting a deliberative theater of the absurd—where illumination met disillusionment.

Consider the pamphlet "Qu'est-ce que c'est la liberté?" penned by the ardent Jean-Paul Marat. This inflammatory treatise fanned the flames of discontent with such fervor that it could almost be tasted in the air—a caustic mixture of ink and blood seeping into the very soil of Paris. Marat's fervor for radical democracy revealed a mind seduced by the promise of unrestricted reason, yet increasingly ensnared in its own contradictions. Marginalizing those who dared question this new order, Marat transformed print into a weapon; the very existence of dissent became treason in his eyes. As readers absorbed the revolutionary fervor of his proclamations, they scarcely could acknowledge the paradox—a call for liberty that imprisoned thought.

Yet, pamphlets weren't just figments of a singular revolutionary vision; they acted as the very pulse of a society wrestling itself free from frivolity and tyranny. Each pamphlet was an artifact, an urgent cog in a sprawling machinery of social upheaval. Edifying in style yet incendiary in content, they summoned the citizenry to organize, to resist, and ultimately, to envision a new horizon. “L'Ami du peuple” stood not merely as a journal but as a crucible for revolutionary ideology—a linchpin in the explosive rallying cry of a populace disillusioned by the monarchy's antiquated grip.

But what lay beneath the polished surface of these pamphlets? Each one bore the fingerprint of its writer’s unique stance, often embedded with the emotional torments of loss, violence, and the struggle for identity. Take, for instance, the work of Camille Desmoulins, whose pamphlets were a vivid juxtaposition of radicalism and introspection. His was not a call to arms devoid of empathy; rather, it was laced with the palpable sorrow of a France divided. Desmoulins emphasized clarity— “The most excellent Revolution is that which leaves the people the least misery”—invoking an emotional resonance that transcended mere rhetoric. Yet even he would later succumb to the guillotine's call, illustrating the perilous fragility of ideological purity amid the wreckage of moralistic fervor.

As ideological fervor surged, pamphlets also served as a mirror reflecting the glorious and gruesome realities of the Revolution. They chronicled its exhilarating rise while foreshadowing its deadly plunge into chaos. Under the skin of each historical moment lay the grotesque irony of revolutionary aspiration: a struggle for autonomy that birthed a new tyranny with the Reign of Terror. The very writers who penned visions of liberty—like Maximilien Robespierre—would find themselves grappling with the darker hues of their own creation. As the gears of violence turned, the pamphlets transformed from vessels of ideology to instruments of condemnation. The ink would bleed, perpetuating divisions; the line between revolutionary and counter-revolutionary grew thin, often obscured in a frenzy of accusations.

Amidst this turmoil, the pamphlet became more than an artifact—it evolved into a symbol of ideological subversion. In the hands of figures like Louise de Kéralio, women writers emerged as not only participants but potent challengers in the tumultuous narratives. They fiercely championed rights, demanding a narrative space unencumbered by male dominance. Kéralio's insistence on women's voices resonated against the backdrop of an unfolding myth: how could a Revolution that advocated for universal rights remain blind to half its population? It exposed the hypocrisy entrenched in radical ideals and spawned debates that would echo through the ages.

Yet, beneath the surface of coalitions and camaraderie existed a schism, punctuated by the realization that revolutionary ideals had veered dangerously close to stagnation. As pamphlets inundated the burgeoning public sphere, the ideological battles morphed into a sordid performance. Each writer sought not merely to inform but to dominate. Here lay the heart of tragedy—what sang as righteousness quickly diminished into warfare of words, where the currency of truth blurred into the realm of conjecture.

A poignant example rests in the work of Pierre-Sylvain Maréchal, who wielded pamphlets infused not with frenzied zeal but with a dispassionate dissection of society's failings. His essays laid bare the ideological tensions, capturing the scent of bloodshed mingled with hope. Maréchal's stance questioned the burgeoning mythos of the Revolution, passionately asserting that in the quest for equality, the vision had succumbed to authoritarianism cloaked in idealism. His narratives wove through sin and salvation, challenging readers to confront the omnipresent human frailties embedded in the revolutionary ethos.

The last act of this tragic tableau unfolded as the Revolution spiraled into a cacophony of despair. With the establishment of the Directory and the creeping shadows of authoritarianism, the pamphlet as a medium struggled to maintain its grip on ideological purity. What was once a vessel for enlightenment became contaminated with fear, its pages stained by the blood of dissenters. The insatiable appetite for control subsumed the initial visions of liberty, resulting in a counter-revolutionary mindset that sought to liquidate every vestige of original thought.

As the sun set on the fervor of the Revolution, the pamphlets that once fueled dreams of a utopian future now lay scattered like autumn leaves—signals of a paradoxical legacy. No longer merely instruments of dissemination, they had grown heavy with the weight of expectation and the rushing tide of betrayal. The very tenets of liberty and equality, so passionately championed, had morphed beneath the relentless scrutiny of a society caught in its contradictions. And yet, in this robust interplay between rancor and aspiration, a new chapter of discourse sprang to life—a martyr's murmur that hinted at resurgence, inciting generations yet unborn to inch closer to the truths obscured in the footnotes of history.

So, what remains woven into this narrative? The pamphlets and polemics of the French Revolution serve as a testament to the paradox of human ambition—a delicate dance between enlightenment and despair, between progress and regression. They echo the remnants of every uprising, every ideal birthed through the ink-stained labor of those who dared to dream. Yet, history warns us: to reclaim the unsung notes of that era is to grapple with the understanding that revolutions are not just fought in the streets; ultimately, they are fought in the minds of the people, where the enduring battle for truth remains the most treacherous endeavor of all.

British and American conspiracy claims

In the sprawling panorama of conspiracy theories, few tales are more intoxicating than those spun around the Illuminati—a name that stirs both dread and fascination. But as the shadows grew long in the late 18th century, a peculiar metamorphosis took place. The allure of a shadowy cabal began to entwine itself with the tumultuous politics of Britain and America, where tumult and trepidation merged into an explosive cocktail of paranoia and ideology. Before history could gain a secure foothold, the suspects were already defined, accusations levied, and the narrative shifted dramatically from lofty aspirations of enlightenment to a darker struggle for sovereignty.

In Britain, an island shaped by revolution's echoes and fearful of the radical ideas imported from France, the Illuminati served as a convenient scapegoat for those unwilling to confront their own domestic discontent. Beneath the polished surface of society lay the rampant unrest of ordinary citizens, feeling forgotten amidst a widening gulf between the aristocracy and the masses. Such dissent was dangerous; the very notion of a societal upheaval threatened the equilibrium of a system built on inherited privilege. Thus, the specter of the Illuminati emerged amidst the discontent—a sinister force invoking dread, a faceless enemy carting forth a wave of revolution to engulf the kingdom.

In 1797, a feverish pamphlet authored by a certain John Robison, a Scottish physicist, draped the growing fears of the British nobility in thick layers of rhetoric. He claimed that the Illuminati had infiltrated every intellect in Europe, turning scholars into agents of chaos. For Robison, it was not merely a matter of ideological betrayal; it was a crude invasion, a subversion of cherished institutions that needed defense. His work resonated through salons and high courts alike, perfuming the air with the scent of terror. But what was it really that sparked this mania?

The Enlightenment had carved a new path for humanity, offering emancipation from dogma and the chains of ignorance. Yet, as ideals spiraled into fervor, fear blossomed as much as hope did. Enlightenment thought brought with it the urgency of dissent; it placed the very pillars of monarchy and established religion into question. Suddenly, men of reason were suspect. Robison's seeming clairvoyance unearthed not just a fanciful enemy but cast shadows upon those who dared to think differently—a self-fulfilling prophecy, where reason became its own adversary in the eyes of the fearful elite.

Across the Atlantic, similar sentiments bubbled to the surface. In America, the promise of a new nation birthed from revolution soon became tainted with distrust. The Founding Fathers themselves, those radical architects of democracy, were now subjects of scrutiny; their very vision could be hijacked by clandestine forces lurking in the shadows, seeking to unravel the fragile fabric of their experiment. Thomas Jefferson, once revered as the champion of enlightenment ideals, faced accusations of collusion with the Illuminati, a label polished and spit-shined by political rivals craving to mar his legacy with whispers of treachery.

Fear of the Illuminati tucked itself tightly into American politics in the early 19th century, where it morphed from a European ghost story into a homegrown boogeyman. This shift to a more localized form of paranoia became emblematic of a nation grappling with itself as factions formed—the rabble versus the orderly, the liberal against the conservative. Let us not forget 1820, when the unfounded accusations of "secret societies" began to emerge in mass discourse, stoking fear of something foreign infiltrating the heart of American democracy. Suddenly, to claim allegiance to any radical idea was to sign a pact with darkness, sought by those who wished to roll back progress into a comforting nostalgia for yesteryear.

Of course, the swirling mists of obscurity surrounding the Illuminati ignited imaginations far and wide. Eager audiences lapped up tales rich with intrigue and moral uncertainty. The perennially inventive Royall Tyler, a playwright and judge, even penned a melodrama entitled "The Contrast" in 1787, which marinated conspiracies with satire. Tyler's characterization of the so-called Illuminati became part of America's early cultural fabric, where the sharp edges of fear were softened by wit but still resonated with foreboding. Here, the theater operated as a crucible, where among the laughter, deeper unrest simmered.

Where the prosperity of early capitalism wove an intricate tapestry of ambition, the threads of anxiety ran parallel. Progress, after all, rested upon fragile assumptions of trust—the currency of a nation built on competing ideologies and dissent. Among the ordinary citizens caught in the throes of emerging capitalism, the shadows of conspiracy served not merely as diversion but as a coping mechanism to confront uncertainty.

As the 19th century unfurled its chapters, the dual specters of American republicanism and British aristocracy remained locked in a dance fraught with nerves. There was Joe Smith in America, who started the Church of Jesus Christ of Latter-day Saints, interpreting angelic visitations in a way that channeled fears of an encroaching conspiracy. His revelations, echoing old fears linked back to Weishaupt, blended the peculiar with the divine, overwhelming the script of rationality until the secular was rife with implications of supernatural intrigues.

In Britain, the rising tide of industrialization exhumed the very seeds of class conflict, planting the paranoid belief that the downtrodden were merely puppets of an invisible hand, twisting their fates in an elaborate dance orchestrated by the Illuminati. The claims consumed ink and paper, conflicting ideologies fighting for supremacy amidst an unfolding social landscape denser than fog—an environment ripe for myth-making.

Ultimately, as the imaginative undercurrents collided with palpable reality, the confluence of British and American conspiracy narratives surrounding the Illuminati began to chip away at the idealism that had once flowed in their veins. What began as fears of subversion morphed into deep-rooted belief systems that relegated rational discourse to the sideline, feeding an insatiable appetite for the shadowy. The meek aspirations of reform and revolution gradually eroded beneath a relentless tide of suspicion and conspiratorial thinking.

And therein lies the tragedy: what began within the enlightened chambers of thought transformed into weapons wielded in political battles, a paradox where the very ideals of liberty birthed an era of fear. Before it all unraveled, the Illuminati metamorphosed from a group of progressive thinkers into a phantasmic adversary haunting the nightmares of both the elite and the populace. The question remains: could it have happened differently?

Early theorists and the rise of Illuminati myths

In the shadowy corridors of Enlightenment thought, where reason and rhetoric danced a perilous waltz, the early theorists laid the philosophical groundwork for the fabrications that would later envelop the Illuminati in layers of myth. These were not just idle dreamers. They were intellectual powerhouses—figures like Voltaire, Rousseau, and Diderot—whose quills ignited fervent debates about freedom, governance, and secretive societies. Yet beneath the polished surface of their writings lurked anxieties that would breed a mythology far richer than their rational ideologies.

In Bavaria, the seeds sown by Adam Weishaupt's fledgling Illuminati took root just as the tensions of the Age of Enlightenment reached fever pitch. The organization emerged from a crucible of secrecy, striving to promote reason but inadvertently inviting speculation. As Weishaupt penned his vision of a more enlightened society, he unwittingly positioned his creation as a fulcrum upon which competing ideologies precariously balanced. The ideal of knowledge as liberation gave rise to another truth—knowledge, especially when cloaked in secrecy, can breed paranoia.

While Weishaupt sought to outthink the world, critics lurked like wolves in the shadows, eager to unveil what they deemed the obscured agenda of these 'enlightened' individuals. The narrative shifted as writers began to tether the Illuminati to plots darker than even their founding ideals. One of the earliest and most infamous theorists, the similarly named adversary of the Enlightenment, Augustin Barruel, spun a web connecting the Illuminati to the very heart of societal upheaval. He pushed the alarming thesis that they orchestrated the French Revolution—a chaotic symphony of bloodshed and ideology gone awry. To Barruel, the Illuminati were puppeteers pulling the strings of history's grandest tragedy, manipulating events from an arcane distance.

Imagine Paris, 1797, an echoing chamber for revolutionary fervor and fear. Barruel's pen moved rapidly, chronicling conspiracies that escalated with each passing chapter. He called upon images of shadowy generals marshaled by Weishaupt to stifle the rise of monarchs and faith. This vision of the Illuminati left an indelible mark as it leapt from pamphlets into discussions, infecting the collective imagination with an insatiable desire for hidden truths. The story of the Illuminati morphed from mere political philosophy to harbingers of chaos, succumbing to the thrilling allure of the secret society genre—one where the boundaries between reality and myth blur precariously.

In the decades that followed, other voices joined the cacophony. John Robison, a Scottish Mason equally concerned by the idea of a cabal subverting societal norms, advanced the notion of an Illuminati infiltration into Masonic lodges. For him, the existence of this twisted fraternity stood as an affront to truth and civility. As his words spread, they solidified a fear that resonated deeply within societies still reeling from revolutionary change. Readers clung to notions of ideologies cloaked in clandestine meetings and veiled intentions. What were these secret societies if not a reflection of their own hidden fears—a glimpse through a warped mirror of societal decay?

The potency of these narratives did not go unnoticed. By the dawn of the 19th century, a menagerie of conspiracy theories blossomed, feeding off the embers ignited by Weishaupt's Illuminati. Fiction and fact intertwined, reeled tightly into a coil of suspicion. A reader perusing these texts could feel their heart race, ensnared by the vivid depictions of clandestine meetings and cryptic symbols—esoteric knowledge lay tantalizingly out of reach yet burned brightly in the imagination.

The illuminating irony of this era lies in how each new theorist compounded the anxiety that preceded them. Mistrust wafted through the streets like an acrid smoke; it wafted through salons and taverns alike, fueled by both fear and fascination. The intersection of ideology and reality became a battlefield, where revelation was both protective armor and a curse, breeding further myth. Readers were left grappling not just with the specter of the Illuminati, but with their own interpretations of moral decay, the price of progress, and the eroding power of truth.

In late 18th-century America, the mythosphere thickened. Lists of conspirators emerged laced with names of Founding Fathers, as if these architects of liberty had adorned themselves in the sacrilege of another kind of freedom—one freed from scrutinizing eyes. The mythology matured, becoming a call to arms for factions both fervent and deranged. Tom Paine, who once championed reason, found himself ensnared in the fascinating yet treacherous web of accusations that looped him into the shadowy organization.

The thrill of the conspiracy tugged at the hearts of men and women, drawing them to the myth of the Illuminati as a way to navigate their own uncertainties. As revolutions—the American and French, in particular—unspooled towards chaos, the very concept of enlightenment became suspect. The idealism of the Enlightenment, its confidence in progress and rational thought, now faced its antithesis in the imagined threat of those who purported to wield knowledge as a weapon.

Yet for all the fears they invoked, these tales presented the opportunity to reflect on the human condition itself. Beneath the surface of cloak-and-dagger stories, the discourse about truth and power swirled. It posed a troubling inquiry into how far one could go in the name of enlightenment, a query that plagues societies to this day. Are we, too, participants in our own narratives of revelation? Do we trade reason for wild speculation, exchanging one set of ideologies for another, just as our ancestors did?

The early theorists of Illuminati myths did more than create tales of conspiracy—they ignited a fascination that continues to pulse within the public consciousness, a trepidation entwisted in the promise of hidden knowledge. As history burgeoned with these narratives, its resonance paved the road for later generations to ponder the shadows lurking beneath both overt and covert histories. The myth of the Illuminati became less about the organization and more a reflection of our deepest fears—a mirror to the turbulent waters of revolution, ideology, and the consequences of unchecked ambition. Before it all unraveled, these theorists had crafted a legacy compelling enough to transcend time, inviting us to confront the terrifying question of who really pulls the strings in the grand theatre of human affairs.

Chapter 7: The Global Myth Machine

Linking Illuminati to revolutions worldwide

The shadow of the Illuminati stretches far beyond its Bavarian origins, a spectral thread weaving through the fabric of global revolutions. As empires crumbled and the old orders faltered, the myth of the Illuminati burgeoned in the minds of those yearning for change. Beneath the polished surface of stories told in candle-lit parlors and radical pamphlets lay the truth that this secret society—often dismissed as a parlor trick of conspiracy theorists—was emblematic of an era grappling with upheaval and rebirth. History does not merely observe the past; it dances with its specters, demanding our attention.

In France, the fire of the Revolution was ignited not solely by the cries for liberty, equality, and fraternity but by an ideological fervor that echoed deeply within the works and actions of Enlightenment thinkers. Voltaire, Rousseau, and their ilk wielded ideas like swords; their writings cut through the chains of feudalism, exposing the rot of monarchical privilege. Insurgents who stormed the Bastille were not just petty criminals but disciples of radical thought, eager to dismantle the entire edifice of authority. And there, amidst the chaos, the shadows of the Illuminati flickered—a beacon for those who sought to reengineer society.

As revolutionary fervor took root in France, the specter of secret societies gained potency. Rumors began to swirl, claiming that the Illuminati sought to orchestrate the tumult from behind the curtain. These whispers fed the imagination as the guillotine sliced through the air, where political ideas met the blood of the betrayed and the idealistic. Were the Illuminati agents of progress, or merely opportunists watching the world burn? The answer lay hidden in the heart of the revolution—a twisted grappling with an elusive ideology, which pivoted dangerously between utopia and dystopia.

Across the Channel, the fervor found another expression. England was not immune to the revolutionary tide that swept through Europe, but it took distinct forms—first in the radical pamphleteering of Thomas Paine and later in the violence of the Luddite movement. Here, in the dark mines and smoking factories where workers toiled, a palpable sense of injustice fueled a longing for a shared vision. As strikes erupted and protests raged, a pop-up counterculture emerged, echoing the Enlightenment's challenge to authority. Amidst these movements, the image of the Illuminati persisted as it was invoked by the ruling elite to consolidate their power, framing dissent as evidence of a conspiratorial contagion.

Paine's prophetic words warned of tyranny as he championed visions of democracy. The ancient intelligentsia morphed into new social architects—replacing the monarchs of yesteryear with something altogether more democratic yet fragile. Would-be revolutionists began to conflate liberty with chaos, and liberty with factionalism—a heady brew of ambition that risked mutual destruction. The Illuminati myth found itself at once vilified and embraced, crafting a duality that mirrored the struggle between innovation and fear.

But the narrative of the Illuminati did not rest easily; it spread like wildfire to the shores of the Americas. With the American Revolution lifting up the banner of self-determination, the idea of an enlightened elite secretly shaping history turned into a battle cry for both revolution and oppression. The likes of George Washington and Thomas Jefferson may have spoken of liberty, yet in hushed taverns and parchment-choked studies, the musings of Weishaupt felt disturbingly familiar. Was the Illuminati guiding the hands of the Founding Fathers, ensuring that they would coax the ultimate semblance of democracy into existence?

The answer is less about the existence of an Illuminati thread and more about what it represented—a yearning for agency amid chaos. Against the constant backdrop of war and instability, the Confederation of Society grew, where clandestine gatherings rotated around not just revolutionary ideology but also power struggles masked under the guise of fraternity. Each secret meeting sought to fathom the will of the people while simultaneously grappling with its vicious contradictions, antepenultimate in the circles of conspiracy.

From the tumult of the Americas, the whisper of revolution echoed to Latin America. Figures such as Simón Bolívar rose from the ashes of colonial rule, fueled by dreams of freedom. However, the revolutionary zeal was often muddied by factions and infighting. In Caracas, the winds of change met the swift suspicion of the Illuminati's influence, just as the colonized sought to throw off the chains of Spanish governance. Spanish authorities depicted pro-independence figures as pawns of an international conspiracy, blending the veritable threat to their thrones with a touch of familiar fear: the specter that a shadowy elite might be marshaling the chaos for their own gain.

While the myth solidified the paranoia among monarchies fearing uprisings, it simultaneously empowered those wishing to establish their own utopias, intelligent of the dangers yet drawn to the fires of revolution. The contrasting responses to the perceived threat of the Illuminati bore witness to the dialectic relationship between ideology and reality. In the best of times, ideals of freedom met collective action; in the worst, factional divides tore through the hearts of nations.

As revolutions spread, the narrative of the Illuminati morphed into a global story—a tale woven of fears that transitioned seamlessly from one revolution to the next. Each insurrection found its lineage in this cryptic acknowledgment of the potential for systemic collapse. Whether championing the ideals of the Enlightenment or demonizing them as clandestine manipulation, societies grappled with the challenge of revolution's unyielding duality.

In reflecting upon the fabric of revolutions—their triumphs and inevitable missteps—it is crucial to heed the warnings buried deep within the myths we tell ourselves. The truth often lies not in the concrete happenings of clandestine gatherings or the manipulation of ideological rhetoric, but rather in the messy intersections of hope, despair, and humanity's relentless quest for meaning. To overlook the footnotes of history is to strip away the nuances that tether us to our understanding of the past—in this case, the myth of the Illuminati serves as a portal, ever demanding that we wrestle with the profound ramifications of true revolutionary potential.

Let us stand vigil, ready to explore the deep abyss of our historical narratives, for there, we might find reflections of the Illuminati's legacy—layers of illusion, truth, and myth intertwining perpetually as the wheels of revolution roll onward into futures unknown.

The Illuminati as a political and cultural weapon

The Illuminati's legacy is often painted in shades of shadow and conspiracy, lurking menacingly as a specter that haunts the annals of political discourse. Yet, at its inception, this so-called secret society was less about clandestine control and more about an audacious experiment—a daring ideological proposition. A clutch of enlightenment thinkers could hardly fathom that their intellectual reverie would be repurposed into a political and cultural weapon, morphing into a global myth that thrived on the paranoia of the masses.

Beneath the polished surface of historical glamour, Weishaupt and his circle were not insidious puppeteers; they were utopians. The Bavarian professor sought to unlock the minds of men, to rid society of dogmas nagging at the roots of reason. Yet only a few years after the Illuminati sprouted, the narrative would swiftly shift; it became a tool, fear soaked and disingenuous, exploited by those who understood the gravitational pull of myth in a rapidly changing world.

With the French Revolution as a backdrop, the mythos of the Illuminati morphed into a dual-edged sword. On one end, they represented the anarchic spirit of enlightenment—a clarion call for revolution, equality, and a break from monarchic chains. On the other, they bloomed as bogeymen, an unintentionally crafted weapon wielded by reactionary forces desperate to maintain their grip on power. The fertile soil of chaos ignited fears of subversion, and the whispers grew louder— “They are among us. They seek to destroy civilization as we know it.” For the ruling classes, the Illuminati served as an inconvenient truth for the revolutionary fervor of the masses: their calls for freedom were systematically pigeonholed as the machinations of typified secretive conspirators.

We wear our ideological constructs like armor. Historical narratives often transform into an arsenal wielded to shape culture and governance. Consider the chilling pamphlets and political treatises circulated in post-revolutionary France, which delightfully entwined the Illuminati with images of radicalism gone awry. Churches and monarchies interlaced their survival with these tales—the plotted chaos became the fingerprints on every uprising, every moment of discord. The Illuminati were never a monolithic organization, yet countless heads turned in their direction when chaos erupted, pointing fingers as if in a fevered dream.

Yet the externalizations of fear can never crystallize without an internal affirmation. The belief in such a conspiracy becomes a shared cultural narrative, for it feeds upon the very vulnerabilities that demarcate the human condition. As societies grappled with the birth pangs of modernity, the sense of alienation grew and fear of the unknown deepened. In this climate, fraught with rapid ideological shifts and discontents, you could thread the needle between paranoia and truth with the simplest of aims: a search for meaning. The Illuminati, once a symbol of radical philosophical thought, became a narrative scaffold upon which unprecedented political engenderments were constructed.

How does one account for the weaponization of ideology? When meteoric movements expose fractures in the societal fabric, those in power frantically deploy every tool at their disposal. In America, the Revolution birthed a distinct paradox within the political landscape.

While it championed liberty, it also whispered fearful reminders of loss. The emergent republic wrestled with shadows of factionalism; Federalists and Anti-Federalists found their battle lines dreadfully defined. Fearing the rise of Jacobinism, born of the French experience, American leaders conjured up the specter of shadowy conspirators plotting to ensnare the nation in an abyss. They harnessed the very fear that the Illuminati inspired, reifying it as a political weapon that could rally a fearful populace—one born from revolutionary zeal.

But let's not forget the performers in the narrative: authors and pamphleteers, those deftly wielding the pen like a rapier. William Russell's inflammatory writings accused revolutionary societies of harboring ties to the Illuminati, claiming the very health of the Republic was curbed by its malign influence. Within these printed pages lay the ground for a frenetic brand of cultural warfare—one that breached the gap between reality and the specter of a fabricated historical fear. These cultural narratives did not merely threaten the progress of ideologies; they threatened the soul of the nation.

As the 19th century became a theater for burgeoning ideologies that would reshape the world—socialism, republicanism, and liberalism—the ghost of the Illuminati materialized not as a formal organization, but as a pervasive permutation of our psyche, casting long shadows on the political debates of every nation. They represent a latent fear of the collective, a gripping anxiety that modernity could tear apart the seams of the moral fabric. Social thinkers and revolutionaries—including Marx—exploited this fear, engaging in a double dance. They acknowledged revolutionary necessity while wrestling with the inertia of the specter that haunted them. Solvable issues morphed into ideological battles where fear reigned supreme; the Illuminati became synonymous with radicalism wholly untethered from its intellectual origins.

The cultural weaponization was not confined to Europe or America; it traveled across the oceans, bleeding into the colonies. An illustration comes to mind from the Caribbean in the early 1800s amidst enslaved uprisings. Here, the myths of the Illuminati were smuggled into whispers of revolt, swirling around the hopes of the oppressed. The army of discontent sought not just the overthrow of chains, but universal emancipation. Those frightened of quotidian revolts launched salvos of propaganda that labeled liberators as agents of the Illuminati—a tactic intended to quell the flames of revolt under the guise of protecting order.

To unearth the duality of this narrative is to reckon with a nearly Sisyphean task. The Illuminati transcended mere history to become an ideological chameleon reflecting society's every fear and ambition. They inspired both the revolutionary aspirations of men and the zealous backlash of tyrants alike. Their very existence became a metaphor—a battleground where idealism met a disillusioned reality.

So, what remains when the dust settles? The Illuminati had no blueprint for global domination nor an opus of tyranny to cast forth. Instead, they inhabit the annals of political discourse as a dynamic chimerical entity—an ethereal construct perpetually reshaped in the language of fear and hope, of conspiracy and liberation. One cannot simply place a label on this phenomenon; it is a reflection of humanity's deepest aspirations and gravest fears.

Before it all unraveled, the Illuminati thrived not merely in the sepulchers of history but as an ongoing conversation about power, identity, and the quest for meaning. They remind us keenly that in the dance of ideology, the most potent weapon is often the one invented by collective imagination. In the shadows of myth, we confront the duality of our existence, where both chains and liberation carve out paths for generations to come.

Why the myth grew beyond the facts

The myth of the Illuminati didn't simply emerge from a void; it unfolded within the threads of a society rife with paranoia, revolution, and the unquenchable thirst for control. As Enlightenment ideals clashed with Old World traditions, unsettling tensions brewed. To understand why the myth grew beyond the facts, we must first peel back the layers of history, examining how a group of earnest scholars transformed into the specters haunting the corridors of power.

Beneath the polished surface of Enlightenment thought lay a profound anxiety. The new ideas of liberty, equality, and reason gnawed at the foundations of monarchies and established churches. Across Europe, men and women whispered of secret cabals and shadowy figures conspiring against the status quo. Enter Adam Weishaupt, a brilliant but often misunderstood professor attempting to advance human thought through radical education and the mentorship of young minds. His Bavarian society, the Illuminati, initially aimed to champion rational discourse and safeguard Enlightenment values from the excesses of dogma. Yet, as with many transformative movements, ambition tainted the trajectory of purpose.

When Weishaupt first organized the Illuminati in 1776, only a handful of individuals populated its ranks. Characteristically, they sought to elevate knowledge over ignorance, reason over superstition. Yet, with each clandestine meeting and whispered decree, the alarm bells rang louder. Beneath the low rumble of academic discourse, a paranoia gathered—one fed not only by royal sirens that warned of treachery but by those who sensed the threat such ideas posed to their very existence.

The irony is rich: to challenge oppression, the Illuminati transformed into a symbol of it. Stories began circulating about their nefarious plots, fueled by fears of change that gripped an unstable continent. Weishaupt himself never envisioned a world where shadows became more powerful than light, yet here we are, marking the moment history lost its grip on fact.

Consider the publication of the so-called "Bavarian Illuminati" documents, purported leaks that claimed exposure of plots to undermine religious and political systems. It's worth noting that these alarming revelations came at a time when the French Revolution was brewing, a maelstrom of radical ideas and bloody opposition to monarchic tyranny. The emerging revolutionary spirit found a perfect scapegoat in the Illuminati, a moniker thrown like a pebble into a lake, rippling outwards with eager zeal. For those shaken by sociopolitical upheaval, the notion of powerful, secretive forces pulling strings proved irresistible—a fantastical explanation for a world spiraling into chaos.

Before it all unraveled into the relentless torrent of conspiracy, we must confront the specter of fear that served not only to create the myth but to magnify it. The masses, drinkers of both hope and dread, imbibed the narrative with frenzied immediacy. We saw Enlightenment values warped into weapons wielded against those who espoused them. The Illuminati now hovered like phantoms, whispering to every public figure, pulling every string. In the minds of many, this fraternity—the very harbinger of reason—was now a face behind every ideological plot.

Yet, the stage upon which this grand drama played out was not limited to the thinkers and revolutionaries of Europe. As the myth took root, it crossed oceans, embedding itself in the fertile soil of American exceptionalism. The United States was born amid dreams of freedom, yet the newfound nation carried its own fears—of tyranny, of elitism, of conspiracy. The writings of some of its founders reflected a profound belief in the necessity of transparency and vigilance against corruption. But in a land where every citizen saw themselves as a player in the grand narrative, it didn't take long for the whispers of the Illuminati to migrate from Europe to the youthful streets of Philadelphia and beyond.

Abraham Lincoln felt the weight of these paranoia-laden whispers in the years leading up to the Civil War. A nation already grappling with its identity suddenly found itself embroiled in shadowy narratives of treason, with accusations of Illuminati involvement surfacing amid the chaos. Those in power succumbed to the allure of a simplistic explanation for complex realities, grasping at the notion of an orchestrated betrayal, thereby fanning the flames of discord. The myth no longer merely lingered in hushed conversations but was thrust into the public consciousness—transforming the Illuminati from a club of philosophical debate to a malignant force lurking within the fabric of American society.

But of course, the Illuminati myth didn't stop there. In the late nineteenth and early twentieth centuries, as societies began to mechanize and modernize, the seeds of pessimism and fear germinated into a full-blown conspiracy industry. Writers and theorists seized upon this narrative—a badge of honor for the paranoid and a revenue stream for the sensationalists. It was no longer merely academic; it was populist entertainment, a seductive tale that had dug its talons into the collective psyche.

By the time the twentieth century rolled around, the myth had become a potent tool of disinformation—a weapon employed by totalitarian regimes, secret societies, and cultural critics alike to mold perception, vilify adversaries, and rally supporters. The Illuminati morphed into a convenient scapegoat for every apposite anxiety. Like a riptide, the myth drew divers deep into treacherous waters, where discernment became drowned among the currents of conspiracy.

Yet, perhaps the most unsettling aspect remains the resonance of the myth with contemporary fears. The digital age, forged in a crucible of interconnectedness, has both amplified and compounded historical anxieties. Where there once were pamphlets and scrolls, now there are tweets and hashtags. The allure of hidden knowledge remains intoxicating, and in the age of misinformation, we once again find ourselves trapped in the fray, casting aspersions blindly—a collective holding firm to the narrative of the Illuminati as if clinging to a lifebuoy in a stormy sea.

So, why did the myth grow beyond the facts? Because beneath the anxiety of change, the desire for clarity molded an erratic, distorted reflection of truth, where darkness offered the comforting simplicity of an answer, no matter how fantastical. The ghost of the Illuminati lingers, not because of any tangible power but because of our innate need for understanding in a world that often leaves us anxiously adrift. And so, we confront history—driven to search the footnotes, to question the narrative, all the while wrestling with the remnants of our own shadows.

Chapter 8: Separating Fact from Fiction

What we know from archives

The story of the Illuminati, like the chaotic interplays of light and shadow in a forgotten attic, beckons to be uncovered within the confines of dusty archives. In the heart of this grand narrative lies not just legendary figures dressed in cloaks at midnight gatherings, but a confluence of ideas, aspirations, and the existential unraveling typical of revolutionary fervor. To approach the historical fabric of the Illuminati, we must delve deeply—not merely skimming the surface where conspicuous truths lie, but plunging into the undercurrents that reveal the essence of a society perched precariously on the edge of radical thought.

The Bavarian State Archives holds a treasure trove that could very well rewrite the script of history. Wading through its intricate collections, one uncovers not merely membership lists laced with intrigue but correspondence that reveals an ideological tapestry woven with a certain desperation to effect change in a world teetering on the brink. Moreover, what these documents provide is not the neat conclusion that conspiracy theorists thrive upon but a messier, more complicated reality. Disruptors of thought often navigate murky waters; the Illuminati members—idealists at heart—were embroiled not only in the pursuit of enlightenment but also in the disarray that accompanies unraveling social norms.

Take, for example, the correspondence between Adam Weishaupt and his cohorts during the late 1770s. Here, Weishaupt, expressing a blend of radical optimism and veiled paranoia, implores his followers to remain vigilant in their quest for enlightenment. "Philosophy must be freed from the chains of superstition," he declares, fervently advocating for a rebirth of intellectual exploration. Yet, beneath this dialogue of brilliance lurks an undercurrent of fear—fear that the world they sought to change was slipping out of their grasp even as they sought to reshape it. It was a paradox: the more they theorized, the more they felt the ground shift beneath them.

As we probe deeper into the archives, it becomes evident that the concept of secret societies was not an embellishment but an echo of a common zeitgeist—a reaction to ancient hierarchies collapsing in the face of Enlightenment ideals. Alongside the Illuminati's documents, we find records of other groups, such as the Rosicrucians and Freemasons, tracing the tributaries of shared aspirations and intellectual rebellion. Each organization jockeyed for its place in the shadowy dialogue of revolution, but they shared a common thread: the belief that enlightenment could indeed craft reality if only the right methods were wielded.

Yet, what emerges from these records is a portrait not just of men driven by ambition, but of individuals caught in webs of their own making. The archives reveal a spiraling descent into paranoia and misplaced trust, with letters that recount betrayals and fractures that would eventually bleed into the public consciousness. The Illuminati, it seems, was not immune to human frailty—a fact largely ignored in the sweeping narratives that paint them as invulnerable puppeteers behind the world stage. Before it all unraveled, Weishaupt faced dissent from within, whispers of betrayal echoing in the very chambers intended for radical thought. Their ideology was simultaneously their greatest ally and their most significant vulnerability.

Perhaps more startling than the betrayals were the cultural repercussions stemming from these clandestine gatherings. Within the pages of the archives, moments reveal how influence was exerted upon the likes of European thinkers and even political frameworks. The actions of the Illuminati rippled through time, shaping narratives from the Revolutionary War to the burgeoning ideas of democracy across the globe. Contrary to the notion of an omnipotent cabal, what emerges is a collective endeavor—each member intertwined in a quest for evolution in thought, desperately clawing towards a future that most could only imagine in fevered dreams.

Consider the redacted pages which hint at unexplained tensions—a particularly cryptic reference to the "Voice of the People," an initiative aimed at harnessing public sentiment. It paints a vividly precarious picture: members clashed over how best to engage with the masses while grappling with the very real fear of persecution. The desire for power directly opposed their aspirations of enlightenment, as they found themselves caught in the gravitational pull of elitism even as they sought the elevation of society itself.

However, these accounts can mislead, leading us into the sprawling maze of myth. Amid the raw data—names, dates, and events—lies a crucial distinction: the context in which these revelations were made. Archives unveil a duality, illuminating that the fervor of belief can similarly dictate narrative; history is often written by those who win, and the Illuminati were subjects of posthumous mythologization. With its depiction as either a nefarious brotherhood or a band of altruistic philosophers, it becomes clear that constructs around their identity have oftentimes contrived against their actual beliefs.

Moreover, amidst the richness of their own correspondence, we see the breaks in ideology—disguised intent and half-truths whispering behind the drapery of ambition. Some members feared that their own success might inadvertently lead to tyrannies no better than those they sought to dismantle. One might imagine Weishaupt mapping out an ethical structure of governance in his studies, only for those plans to saturate with moral ambiguity like an ink blot on parchment. Herein lies the crux of exposure; the very existential ideologies they championed sowed their discontent.

But as you sift through the annals of their existence, consider: what lies beyond these archives? What does it reveal about us—our continual struggles for control, our intent to shape reality, to transfer ideology into tangible reprisal? The Illuminati's tale, a microcosm of larger societal urges, draws us into a deep reflection on the human condition—our ability, and perhaps our compulsion, to believe in an order that transcends the chaos of our lives.

Thus, as we emerge from the shell of the archives, it's essential to carry with us the refracted truths layered beneath the glossy varnish of legend. The Illuminati's true story intricately punctuates the itch for enlightenment with the scars of ideological confrontation, all the while reminding us that history—our history—is fraught with contradictions. Hence, we must engage rigorously with what the archives unveil, holding fast to reason, curiosity, and the never-ending quest for understanding. What are we building around ourselves today that may one day require the same examination? And as always, should we dare to dream beyond the horizon constructed by others, we must remember to check our own footnotes, lest we cease to find ourselves grounded in reality.

What was invented by enemies

The curtain rises on a peculiar theatrical production in the mid-18th century. The players are not who they appear to be, and the audience, like so many of us today, is largely oblivious to the true nature of the show. At its center stands a society birthed from revolutionary zeal—the Bavarian Illuminati, conjured in the imagination of Adam Weishaupt. Yet the very energies that spurred its inception gave rise to a far more compelling narrative, one spun not by its members but by its adversaries. Before it all unraveled, this society became the dark mirror reflecting humanity's greatest fears and aspirations.

Weishaupt's order was born out of a genuine desire for enlightenment, steeped in Enlightenment ideals. The young professor sought to challenge the forces of superstition and oppressive governance that haunted Europe in the aftermath of the Age of Reason. Illuminism, in its nascent form, celebrated the pursuit of knowledge and the dismantling of tyrannical structures. But this quest for wisdom sparked alarm instead of applause, igniting a smoke screen of suspicion. What we must grapple with now is not just who the Illuminati were, but who they were accused of being—an enterprise of intrigue, coercion, and conspiracy.

Enemies help shape our stories as surely as protagonists. Just as the Illuminati motored through the dusty salons of Bavaria, a coterie of royalist and clerical foes—a veritable enemy ensemble—construed a nightmarish plot that would haunt the order long after its dissolution. These detractors wielded their pens like swords, launching tirades in pamphlets and voluminous treatises that branded the Illuminati as nefarious puppeteers bent on world domination. Take, for instance, the alarmist screeds of Father

Augustin de Barruel—a conspiracy theorist before conspiracy theories were even a spark in the social imagination. This Jesuit priest painted Weishaupt as not merely a misguided academic, but rather a demagogue seeking to subvert the natural order, disrupt the foundations of society, and orchestrate the decline of Christianity itself.

Such incendiary language flourished in the artful hands of adversaries, creating a rift between ideation and manifestation. The fear that resonated in these writings spoke directly to the anxieties of a populace drenched in the realities of their time—a time of revolutions, assassinations, and the ceaseless grappling for liberty across Europe. Here lies the irony: what the Illuminati intended as a sanctuary for rational thinkers was transmogrified into a specter of fear, with the very act of their creation birthing a mythology stronger than its origins.

Let us descend into the murky waters of one specific fabrication—the notorious assertion that the Illuminati were behind the French Revolution. The notion clung to the air like a heavy fog, seeping into the consciousness of those who sought any explanation for the chaos that engulfed Paris in 1789. Who could witness the bloodied streets and ascendant guillotine without seeking the hand of a hidden cabal orchestrating it all from the shadows? The truth, however, was far more pedestrian. Few if any Illuminati members were involved in those early upheavals; as Time would so relentlessly show, revolutions are seldom the child of one mind or group. Yet, this fragile tapestry of conjecture lent itself to the development of a narrative that verified the fears of many.

Before the truth could be lauded, it had to be sacrificed on the altar of paranoia. The more potent the fear, the greater the willingness to imbibe the wildest fabrications. The hand of the Orient, the whispers of the Bolsheviks, the undefined dealings of Freemasons and their alleged connection to the Illuminati—they intertwined in a dizzying ballet of conspiracy that, fed by enemies, left the origins of Weishaupt's endeavor gasping for air, lost amid a cacophony of intended chaos and real terror.

But one cannot speak of the enemies of the Illuminati without interrogating their motives. Fear is a potent weapon—it sharpens the mind but can quickly wield chaos as its accompaniment. Opponents of Weishaupt gathered courage by constructing narratives that fused fact with fiction, forging them into destructive weapons of social control. By enshrining the Illuminati in their rhetoric, they found a fitting scapegoat that could account for discontent, instability, and economic trepidation.

Here is where history demands our scrutiny: could it be that the enemies of the Illuminati were inadvertently preserving a kernel of their truth? In their fervor to demonize, they laid bare the real fears eluding their understanding—fears carried by ordinary citizens as they witnessed monarchies crumble and social structures disassemble. Beneath the polished surface of their accusations might some glimmer of recognition exist—that the winds of change indeed beckoned something darker and more unpredictable, something that hinted at the potential upheaval against tyrannical authority. The enemies didn't just invent the Illuminati; they unearthed society's own anxious boundaries—even as they betrayed the very aspirations for which Weishaupt and his followers stood.

The tension between ideology and reality thunders across the timeline of the Illuminati. It should be acknowledged that while Weishaupt stood against a backdrop of reason, his work was filled with contradictions and obfuscations. Though he espoused enlightenment, the methods employed by some members leaned dangerously close toward manipulation and subversion—details quickly seized upon and amplified by opponents desperate to draw lines in the sand. The societies of the Enlightenment were not clean cubes, free from the tarnished hands of human ambition. Ideologies collided, narratives melded, and before long, new myths were birthed with the blood of panic and betrayal.

So where does this leave us? We stand at a crossroads, reaching through the fog of disinformation, seeking clarity in our understanding of events that continue to reverberate through history. The Illuminati—a name that has vibrated in conspiracy-mongering whispers—will always be intertwined with the fears of those wielding the tools of opposition. Truth and fear, woven together, generate a tapestry—a story driven by an eternal conflict, igniting passions, and connecting erosion with ideation.

And here we are, an audience enthralled not by the curtain or the actors, but by the play itself—a ceaseless reverberation of ideology pitted against reality. For unless we lift the darkened veil and inspect the stories told by enemies, we risk surrendering our understanding of history to mere shadows flickering in the firelight. History is frail and potent, crafted in the crucible of conflict. We must refuse to leave it blindly in the hands of those who would sketch dark imaginings upon its canvas. Let us dig deep, go fast, and revisit the hand that constructs narratives anew. Just as the Illuminati thought they could climb above the thoughts of their enemies, we too must reflect on what we choose to believe. The choice is ours.

Why the myth outlived the order

In the annals of history, few organizations have ignited the imaginations of conspiracists and revolutionaries alike as the Illuminati. Born from the cerebral depths of Enlightenment thinking, they were the product of an intellectual ferment that surged through the Bavarian landscape in the late 18th century. But the world remembers them not for what they achieved, or even for their brief flicker of influence, but for what they represented in the shadowy corridors of myth. Before it all unraveled, they had contorted into a dichotomy of truth and fabrication, a duality that would reverberate far beyond their historical existence.

How is it that a clandestine society, which wielded power for barely a decade, could morph into a specter haunting the corridors of our collective consciousness? This phenomenon reveals not only the mechanics of myth-making but also the deep-rooted fears and desires that propel such narratives. Beneath the polished surface of modern conspiracy theories lies a raw human yearning for meaning and connection in a chaotic world. The Illuminati were never omnipotent overseers dictating global policy from the shadows; instead, they emerged as the perfect reflection of societal anxieties. They epitomized a gamble against the rising tide of Enlightenment rationalism, a desire for transcendence over the humdrum limitations of everyday existence.

Take, for instance, the period following the dissolution of the Bavarian Illuminati in 1785. This was no simple knot that one could untangle with ease. As their influence waned under the weight of governmental pressure, the mythos began to absorb the remnants of their legacy. Cultures at once reverent and incredulous sought to fill the yawning chasm left by the absence of a legitimate threat with an imaginative narrative. The opaquer the true story became—the clandestine meetings they held, the ideals they championed—the more fertile the ground became for fantastical interpretations. The Illuminati had not simply vanished; they had transmogrified into something more potent, a potent archetype rife with uncertainty.

Consider one key element underpinning this transition: the fear of the unknown. As societies began to wrestle with seismic shifts brought about by the Industrial Revolution, the Illuminati became a convenient scapegoat for those who felt the old world slipping through their fingers. In an era marked by rampant changes in social structure, rapid advancements in technology, and a new political landscape, those unease-ridden minds clung to the myth of a shadowy elite commanding the present and the future. The Illuminati shifted from a singular organization into a pervasive emblem of control—a culturally rich tapestry woven from paranoia and happenstance.

The narrative weaved around the Illuminati did not arise in a vacuum. It burgeoned in response to concrete fears that pervaded societies shielding their secrets behind wrought-iron gates and sepulchral libraries. Public figures, journalists, and authors began to pump oxygen into this myth. William T. Stead's 19th-century exposé and the clarion calls of writers such as J. Edgar Hoover combined the kernels of truth with exaggerated tales of malevolence. Every fraying edge of the original order became an expansive space where new myths could flourish, drawing lines between ludicrous accusations and plausible affiliations. The Illuminati myth was no longer confined to scholarly circles; it seized the popular imagination, making it ripe for sensationalism.

But why such endurance? To understand its staying power, we must examine our cultural proclivities toward duality—the light and dark, the visible and invisible. The Illuminati became inseparably linked to the fear of losing autonomy in an increasingly mechanized world, where personal agency felt fragile against the machinations of the state. They represented both a captivating narrative of resistance and an easy explanation for the social upheavals that accompanied modernization; they embodied the contrast between an earnest desire for progress and the darker undertones of conspiracy that seem to run parallel to that trajectory.

The tension between ideology and reality unfolded on many fronts in the centuries that followed. The Illuminati's initial role as philosophical provocateurs became subsumed by tales of sinister plots woven into the very fabric of society. The more significant the threat of collectivism and centralization loomed—whether from communism, fascism, or an increasingly powerful state—the further the parallels between the reality of the Illuminati and the myth surrounding them diverged. For every time a new conspiracy approached the stage, echoing earlier fears, the Illuminati myth transformed once more, becoming a malleable construct that could adapt to the changing zeitgeist.

Reflect on the momentous allure of secret societies in our contemporary culture. We immerse ourselves in a focused environment where ideas flex and dart like shadows beneath the surface. There's a magnetic pull toward unveiling secret knowledge and hidden truths, a desire not only to grasp what's obscured but also to assert control over an uncontrollable world. The charade we create—the fear of Illuminati-controlled destinies—cradles a profound social truth: uncertainty prevails. Our history is rife with contradiction, and we often seek refuge in myth as a means to impose order where it appears lacking.

To grasp why the myth persists, we must also peer into the mirror of our psyches. What specters do we summon when we whisper about the Illuminati? They provoke a necessary reflection on our struggles against disenfranchisement and our need for agency. Just as Adam Weishaupt articulated a vision of a more enlightened world, the myth of the Illuminati interacts with our contemporary perceived threats—real or imagined—echoing the cries for transparency in an increasingly opaque society.

In conclusion, the myth of the Illuminati has outlived the order itself due to a convergence of fears, desires, and cultural narratives. Beneath the escalating fabric of conspiracy lies a psychological necessity to counterbalance the relentless tides of uncertainty. In this amalgamation of myth and reality, we find a profound, albeit unnerving, reflection of ourselves—a society groping for clarity in a murky world, ever-attracted to the siren call of the unseen. The Illuminati may have faded into history, but their legend continues, echoing throughout the corridors of time.

Conclusion

The legacy of a short-lived society

The legacy of a short-lived society often occupies a peculiar space within the annals of history. Lesser-known than the revolutions that commandeered popular attention, minor uprisings and revolutionary collectives linger in the shadows, etching unseen marks upon the tapestry of political thought. The Bavarian Illuminati, born in the fertile soil of enlightenment, epitomizes this paradox. Their existence, however fleeting, punctuated the prevailing norms of their time and reverberated through centuries in ways that continue to influence contemporary discourse.

Emerging in 1776, the Illuminati sought to foster a society governed by reason and enlightenment, unfettered by the chains of superstition and authoritarianism. Yet, behind the fervent desire for reform lay frail human aspirations and interpersonal conflicts. Weishaupt's lofty vision quickly became entangled in the very ideologies he sought to dismantle. The society erected an elaborate scaffolding of secrecy and elitism that ultimately undermined its foundational principles. But before it all unraveled, the Illuminati comprised a mosaic of ideas that would seep into contemporary thought, like ink dispersing in water.

Consider the palpable anxiety gripping 18th-century Europe. The echoes of revolution—both in America and France—stirred the masses with a promise of change, igniting a yearning for liberation from the stifling grip of monarchy and dogma. In this charged atmosphere, the Illuminati's brief flicker illuminated pressing questions: What is freedom worth when the innate flaws of humanity betray it? Can a society anchor in secrecy genuinely champion open discourse? Weishaupt, with his fervent belief in rationalist reform, may not have spotted the inevitable fracture creeping into his utopia—one governed less by ideology than by individual ambition and paranoia.

As the Illuminati disbanded and faded into obscurity, the shadows they cast lengthened. The ramifications of their brief existence manifested not merely through historical intrigue but through the growing specter of conspiratorial thought. Their penchant for clandestine meetings and a hierarchical structure paved the way for the imagination of whistle-blowers and conspiracy theorists alike. They became, in a sense, the archetypal antagonist—a phantom cabal operating behind the polished surfaces of respectable society. Beneath the calm veneer of rationality, a darkness thrived, one that would erupt, not in flames, but as a narrative of fear and suspicion that still colors our cultural discourse.

Today, the fear of the hidden is palpable. Consider the proliferation of platforms devoted to conspiracy theories—each woven into the digital fabric of a world increasingly distance from face-to-face communication. People retreat into echo chambers, each revolutionary ideal—once ignited by shared discourse—distorted into a caricature of the paranoid imagination. However, the Illuminati's enduring legacy lies not just in their shadowy reputation but in the perennial reminder that power, elusive as it may seem, always operates in the interplay between the seen and the unseen.

Yet, in examining the legacy of this society, one must ask: What truths remain buried beneath the rubble of their demise? They amplified the call for reason, yet amidst their tightly held ideals, a dissonance arose. Such moments invite reflection on the duality of human nature—the desire for progress colliding with our inclination toward exclusivity. While the Illuminati's mission crumbled, their vision, replete with contradictions, nudged the conversation toward enlightenment ideals that challenged existing power structures.

Decades after their fall, the whispers of the Illuminati were transformed into the fervor of Romanticism—the dream of a world reconstructed on individual liberty, creativity, and polarizing ideas of authority. The irony lies in the fact that the revolutionary impulse sparked by Weishaupt and his compatriots, though never fully realized, laid the groundwork for the very movements of upheaval that would follow. The social experiments of the 19th century—Marx and his critiques of capitalism, the rise of anarchism, and the feminist movements of the antebellum period—would echo the aspirations of a society once consigned to folklore.

In this sense, the Illuminati serve as a nexus for our understanding of dissent, revolution, and societal change. They are a reminder of the unpredictable nature of ideologies attempting to wrestle control from tradition. Although the distinct contours of their message may appear obscured by the passage of time, the legacy of a short-lived society like the Illuminati urges us to interrogate the myths that ensconce modernity.

Ultimately, their rise and fall poses a lingering question: Can we advance past the limitations embedded within our ideologies? As we grapple with this query, the legacy of the Illuminati breathes anew—a call to scrutinize our past and glean wisdom, never foregoing the deeper truth lurking in the margins of history. Instead of seeking refuge in conspiracy, we must engage courageously with the complexities beneath the polished surface of our societies. Only then might we find authentic liberation from the shadows cast by our predecessors.

Why small groups inspire outsized myths

Before the dust settled on the revolutionary fervor of the 18th century, a curious paradox emerged: the very small groups that sought to change the world simultaneously birthed the grandest myths. It's almost poetic, if you think about it. They put forth an ideology, a beguiling promise of enlightenment and progression, yet what history often regurgitates is a confection of conspiracy laced with fear. The Illuminati became the quintessential example of this phenomenon, but they were far from unique. In fact, they were merely the most pronounced embodiment of a broader truth: small assemblies of fervent idealists have an extraordinary capacity to distort reality into myth.

The power of myth thrives in its ability to transcend the mundane. When a handful of people gather to articulate a vision, it's the spark of innovation—not yet a flame—that can ignite the wildest imaginations. Where certainty falters, speculation fills the void. The more tantalizing the idea, the easier it is for the narrative to evolve beyond its modest origins. Picture the Bavarian gathering of Weishaupt and his followers: intellectuals candidly sharing thoughts in candlelit rooms, declaring a new dawn of rationality and freedom. But beneath the polished surface of their dialogue lay undercurrents of paranoia—a fear of persecution and a yearning for acceptance that drove many to cast them as sinister players in a much larger drama than themselves.

As the ideals of the Illuminati seeped into popular consciousness, the original intentions evolved from intellectual pursuit to a shadowy monolith. Suddenly, instead of an assembly of forward thinkers, they were caricatured as puppeteers hiding in the dark corners of society, manipulating events from behind a curtain. This transformation wasn't the result of a single storyteller's pen; it was a collective imagination run amok. Myths flourished because they found fertile ground in societies eager to believe that small groups could indeed wield unimaginable power.

Consider how this phenomenon plays out in more contemporary contexts. In every corner of history, we see small collectives morphing into behemoths of ideology: the Carbonari during Italy's upheaval, the Fabians in England, and even today's tech startups—each has their group of visionaries and conspirators. Each, when viewed through the lens of narrative, is capable of attaining an outsized significance distanced from their actual influence. Why does this happen? Myth thrives on uncertainty and fear—the same emotions that drive public discourse into a frenzy. When the populace faces ambiguity, their minds gravitate toward the dramatic and the unknown, exaggerating the capabilities of these small factions into diabolical plots or miraculous resolutions.

The world is no stranger to disillusionment. When the ambitious visions of small groups falter—when they fail to deliver the utopia they promised—the mythology deepens. The darlings of the Enlightenment may have had revolutionary aspirations, but consider how quickly they became figures of derision, or worse, villainy. This slippage is not confined to the past; we see it today in movements that start with the purest intentions yet dissolve under the weight of their expectations—transforming from catalysts of change into cautionary tales. The fragility of ideals breeds skepticism, and from that skepticism sprouts a rich garden of myths.

Let us not forget that these narratives aren't intrinsically malevolent. They serve a psychological function; they reflect our collective anxieties and desires. They tell us who we are and who we fear. When the Illuminati's name emerged, it wasn't just an invitation to conspiracy; it offered a delicious diversion from the overwhelming truths of political and social dynamics that were impossible to confront. It exposed our yearning for control in a chaotic world, wherein a select few might be attributing significance to events that felt beyond our individual grasp.

In examining how societies construct these powerful myths, we unearth an essential tenet: the mythic potential of small groups—illuminated by the flickering candlelight of shared conviction—often overshadows the reality of their intentions and capabilities. Our challenge is to navigate the labyrinth of these narratives with clarity, resisting the allure to surrender to the captivating tales that beckon us toward the light of conspiracy rather than the authenticity of human experience.

These small groups have the power—both inspiring and terrifying—to frame our understanding of the past. They command attention, whether they wish to or not, and when their whispers echo through the annals of history, they often become deafening roars. By confronting the nuances of these myths and digging deeper into the footnotes that accompany them, we unearth truths more potent than we might dare to imagine. The journey does not end here; rather, it challenges us to question, to dig deep, and to persistently check the footnotes of our history for the clarity that lies beneath the surface.

Bridge to Vol. 4 - The Conspiracy Machine

The secretive halo of the Illuminati—a blend of myth and reality—cast a long shadow, one that has only deepened in the modern era. As whispers of their existence ripple beneath the polished veneer of contemporary society, it becomes increasingly clear that we are not only marveling at remnants of an 18th-century society, but also inextricably threading ourselves into a broader tapestry of conspiracy. Each thread pulls taut, revealing a cross-section of paranoia, aspiration, and the relentless need for power that evokes both the sinister and the sublime. Welcome to the Conspiracy Machine.

What we've unearthed through the past volumes of this tale is not merely the story of a secret society. Rather, it is a dissection of how ideas, once ignited in the minds of radical thinkers, often metamorphose into surreal specters that haunt modern discourse. In the same way Adam Weishaupt harbored aspirations for enlightened change—a vision thwarted by his own creations—contemporary society wrestles with its representatives of ideation and manipulation. Each theory spun like silk on a spider's web connects in intricate patterns, coating our reality in layers of uncertainty and fear. We find ourselves wrestling with questions: Who truly controls the narrative? What power lies in the society of believers, the purveyors of fringe ideologies?

Throughout the course of this exploration, we have seen how revolutionary ideas can inspire movements for freedom on one hand, yet lead to sectarian fanaticism on the other. Consider the fervor of a crowd, incited by the promise of liberation while their minds become entrapped by a conspiracy's siren call. The beauty of revolutionary zeal, sporadically ignited through the ages, can soon devolve into a firestorm of misinformation, as revolutionary fervor fuels paranoia and scapegoating. The inquisitive reader must ask themselves where the line rests between the pursuit of truth and the seduction of conspiracy. Before it all unraveled, what began as enlightenment could easily become the breeding ground for dogma and despair.

As we inch closer to our understanding of the Conspiracy Machine, we witness how the dynamics of fear and control are in an eternal dance. Human history is replete with incidents that underscore these patterns: from the McCarthyite witch hunts to the panicked accusations of secret cabals orchestrating world affairs. Rhetoric morphs into reality, and what seems to originate as rebellion can spiral into zealotry, leading many to portray the Illuminati as an all-powerful puppet master. Yet beneath these explosive myths lies frailty—the fragility of belief itself.

We often overlook the role of those who propagate these beliefs. Therein lies a darker aspect of human nature—the desire for connection in a world that often feels overrun by chaos and mistrust. The Conspiracy Machine often gains traction in societies where inequalities fester and distrust breeds. It finds fertile ground in communities scarred by loss or framed by injustice, leading disillusioned souls to seek solace in unsubstantiated lore. The irony is potent: a quest for truth fueling delusion, gut-wrenching anguish morphing into a blind adherence to narrative.

Yet, there is beauty amidst the chaos. The irony of our age is that, while conspiracy theories may tear at the seams of society, they also draw interest from history's boldest thinkers. They provoke us to interrogate our freedoms, summoning inherent questions of ethics and the nature of governance. The voices of the past beckon us toward a critical inquiry—what does it mean to belong? What structures ensnare our reality, and does confronting those truths empower us?

As we shift our focus from the illuminated shadows of the Enlightenment to the luminescent glow of our own digital age, we find ourselves staring into the maw of the Conspiracy Machine. The next volume will delve deeper, unveiling whether we can transcend the spectral grip of assumptions, to uncover the authentic origins of our fears. By examining the alchemy of belief, we might finally discern not only the dangers of unchecked ideology but the possibility for genuine enlightenment. Prepare yourself, for we are on the cusp of an exploration that could either unravel or illuminate our understanding of the past, resonating into a future weighed down by the legacies we choose to embrace.

Printed in Dunstable, United Kingdom

83139379R00078